Praise for *CoParenting*

"This book, written by a pioneer in the development of Parenting Coordination practice, is a well-crafted, practical guide for parents who have lost their direction in the stormy seas of high-conflict shared custody situations. Dr. Carter demystifies concepts such as coparenting, parenting plans and provides guidance in managing common issues encountered in these complex, challenging situations. It distills and applies the best relevant social science research for parents and professionals alike. This is the book I'll refer parents to who ask the question, 'Should I consider using a Parenting Coordinator?'"

—**MATTHEW J. SULLIVAN**, PhD, Author of *Overcoming the CoParenting Trap*

"There are two things that are extremely important for parents who are separating: they need the knowledge and child-focused tools to formulate their own parenting plan, and they need to have a process to minimize conflict as they move into the future. Debra Carter is contributing a valuable resource for these parents that gives them the practical and child-developmental tools to craft their customized plan, detailed and understandable information about the parenting coordination process which can help them work through serious conflict, and communication skills for keeping on track to avoid future problems. All of this is furnished in language the parents can absorb and identify with, and is underscored with real-life scenarios."

—**HUGH E. STARNES**, Senior Circuit Judge, Fort Myers, FL

"*CoParenting After Divorce* is a clear and simple explanation of Parenting Coordination, as well as a helpful step-by-step guide for separated parents navigating issues from infants to the terrible 2's through older teens. I really liked comparing the Parenting Coordinator to a GPS that helps the parents stay on course – to reach a positive destination for their child(ren). Carter provides lots of research, many examples of parents overcoming conflict, and an abundance of hope. She really knows her stuff! I recommend this book as a helpful introduction to Parenting Coordination for any parent — and professional!"

—**BILL EDDY**, LCSW, Esq., President of High Conflict Institute. He is the author of several books, including *It's All Your Fault: 12 Tips for Managing People Who Blame Others for Everything.*

"Dr. Carter's Guidance for Parenting System gives parents a clear road map for navigating to the most important destination: healthy children. This clear, concise guide spells out proven ways to reduce conflict and keep children's needs a top priority. This book is a 'must have' for divorcing parents."

—**JOANNE PEDRO-CARROLL**, PhD, Clinical Psychologist and Child Specialist; Author, *Putting Children First: Proven parenting strategies for helping children thrive through divorce.*

"One of Dr. Carter's unique gifts is her ability to weed through voluminous research literatures to identify, sort out, and communicate only the most important concepts — in a way that anyone can digest and understand. The 'GPS' concept of this book is an apt and perfect metaphor for how she serves us all by illuminating the most productive paths. Parents will find great value in this book; it is a straightforward and eye-opening but 'easy' read. In my view, a terrific and much-needed contribution!"

—**JAMIE MCHALE**, PhD Director, Family Study Center, University of South Florida

ALSO BY DEBRA K. CARTER

Parenting Coordination:
A Practical Guide for Family Law Professionals

-209 3650

CoParenting After Divorce

A GPS for Healthy Kids

This book introduces the Guidance for Parenting System (GPS), a road map for parents during and after divorce. The GPS is a Parenting Plan that you and your child's other parent can develop and follow on your own or get help through a Parenting Coordinator.

WITHDRAWN

Debra K. Carter, PhD

IJUN 0 8 20..

CRANBERRY PUBLIC LIBRARY
2525 ROCHESTER ROAD, SUITE 300
CRANBERRY TOWNSHIP, PA 16066
724-776-9100

UNHOOKED BOOKS
an imprint of High Conflict Institute Press
Scottsdale, Arizona

Publisher's Note
This publication is designed to provide accurate and authoritative information about the subject matters covered. It is sold with the understanding that neither the author nor publisher are rendering legal, mental health, medical, or other professional services, either directly or indirectly. If expert assistance, legal services, or counseling is needed, the services of a competent professional should be sought. Neither the author nor the publisher shall be liable or responsible for any loss or damage allegedly arising as a consequence of your use or application of any information or suggestions in this book.

Copyright © 2015 by Debra K. Carter
Unhooked Books, LLC
7701 E. Indian School Rd., Ste. F
Scottsdale, AZ 85251
www.unhookedbooks.com

ISBN: 978-1-936268-88-7
eISBN: 978-1-936268-89-4

All Rights Reserved.
No part of this book may be reproduced, transmitted, down-loaded, scanned, decompiled, reverse engineered, or stored in or introduced into any information storage and retrieval system, or distributed in any printed or electronic form or by any means, whether electronic or mechanical, now known or hereinafter invented, without the express written permission of the publisher. Failure to comply with these terms may expose you to legal action and damages for copyright infringement.

Names and identifying information of private individuals have been changed to preserve anonymity.

Library of Congress Control Number: 2014959883

Cover design by Gordan Blazevik
Interior layout by Jeffrey Fuller, Shelfish.weebly.com

Printed in the United States of America

ACKNOWLEDGMENTS

I am eternally grateful to the families who suspended disbelief, opened their hearts and minds and allowed me to be an instrument of positive change in their lives.

Many thanks go to Michael who cheerfully keeps all aspects of life running when I'm absorbed in my work. And to LGM – without you, there would not have been a GPS.

To Chris, Lauren, and Chase

Contents

CHAPTER ONE

Parenting Coordination:

The GPS (Guidance for Parenting System) Model

W hen planning a trip, it's a good idea to know the destination ahead of time. Where are you going? What route do you want to take? Will it be direct, or do you want to take a scenic byway? Where can you get gas, food, or emergency help along the way?

It's the same when planning for your child's future during or after a divorce. Knowing your destination is the most important part of planning. Even if you and your ex, or soon-to-be ex-spouse or partner, cannot agree on much of anything, you can usually agree on where (and what) you want your child to be.

- *"Parker should have a good education."*
- *"Pamela should stay healthy."*
- *"Parker should be a good citizen."*

Agreeing on what you are interested in for your children takes away the "right" or "wrong" from parenting decisions. It changes how you think about parenting. Focusing on your children—what is best for them, even if it may be hard for you—will help ensure that your children reach their destination of healthy, happy adults.

When you are not sure how to get to a certain place, a GPS is a good tool. Enter in the address where you want to go, and the GPS will tell you how to get there, turn by turn. This book will introduce the Guidance for Parenting System, a road map for parents of divorce. The GPS in this case is a Parenting Plan, put in place and monitored by a Parenting Coordinator. (Even if you're not working with a Parenting Coordinator, you can use this book as a resource for parenting after divorce.)

What Does a Parenting Coordinator Do?

A Parenting Coordinator is a professional who helps parents map out the plan for their children during and after divorce. The Parenting Coordinator can be a lawyer, mediator, psychologist, social worker, or mental health professional. This is a person who has gone through special training and is qualified by the court for such work.

Parenting coordination can help families and parents in many ways. Here are some examples:

- Helping parents shift from romantic partners to parenting partners
- Teaching parents how to manage negative feelings in a positive way
- Giving parents and children good communication tools
- Setting up ways to work out conflicts between parents
- Keeping to the court-ordered plan
- Saving legal costs

The Parenting Coordinator works *with* parents, *for* children. The children are the focus.

Let me repeat that: your children are the focus. Not you. Not your ex, as wrong as you feel he is. Not the new stepmother, as wrong as you think she is. Your children are the ones who had no say in the divorce and who need both parents now more than ever.

TRY THIS:

The next time you meet with your ex to talk about plans for your children, take a picture of the children with you. Lay the picture between you and your ex. When you begin to stray off topic, look at the photo and then refocus on your children.

It's about them!

In my work as a Parenting Coordinator, I find that this is the most important step in a parenting plan. Parents who learn to *keep the children as the focus* can, and do, set up good plans for their children—the kind of plans that get your children to their destinations feeling happy and healthy. It can be done. You can do it.

Keeping the children as the focus, in one way, is very easy; in another way, it can be quite hard. It is easy, as a parent, to want the best for your children. That is a natural feeling for a parent. But keeping the children as your focus after divorce often means letting go of anger, hurt, and resentment. That is much harder to do.

When my daughter was three years old, she had a terrible fever. Her doctor had given her medicine to take and told me to bathe her in cool water as needed. The medicine helped a little, but her fever raged on throughout the night. I stayed up all night, bathing her to cool her off, rocking her in my arms, and feeding her ice chips. It was easy then to focus just on her. I would never have thought of putting her in bed and going to sleep myself until she was better.

But in a divorce, there is no medical emergency demanding that you stay focused on your children. You might be hurting so much yourself that it's hard to think clearly. Now is the time, however, to focus on your children, just as I did on that long night with my daughter. Once a parenting plan is in place, you can relax and follow the plan.

The parenting plan will include you and your ex (or soon-to-be ex), as well as other people important to your children. A grandmother may take care of the children after school, and so is an important part of their lives. An aunt may drive the children to karate lessons. A nephew may coach your son's soccer team and be a role model. Your ex may have remarried, and a stepmother is now part of the plan. Everyone has their part to play in making sure that your children reach their final destination.

The parenting plan lets you know what to expect. It will change as your children grow, since what they need today will not be the same as what they need in five years. The plan, like the GPS, guides you turn by turn. And, if you make a wrong turn, you and the Parenting Coordinator can "recalculate" the plan, just as a GPS figures out a new route after you get off course.

The Phases of Parenting Coordination

Parenting coordination usually happens in three phases. The first is redefining the family. An important fact to know in this process is that all families change—with or without divorce. Children grow up and move out. A grandmother dies. A father gets a new job and the family moves to another town. Change is a normal part of family life. Every family will look different at different times. What happens in divorce is that the family may now have a dad, a stepdad and one mom or a mom, a stepmom, and a dad. This becomes the new "normal."

To children, normal can come more easily than you think. This is especially true if parents calmly act as if normal really is . . . normal. I once worked with a ten-year-old girl whose mother had died two years before. When the girl was helping her dad fill out forms for middle school, she noticed a section with check boxes for "Parents: Married, Single, Divorced, or Widowed." The girl complained that she wanted to mark the form "divorced" rather than "widowed" because divorce was more normal to her. "All my friends have divorced parents. None of them have to check widowed on the form. Why can't I be like the other kids?"

In this first phase, normalizing divorce is followed by parents setting up goals for their children. These common interests—health, education, and so on—become the destinations to set in the GPS parenting plan. Parents move from thinking of right and wrong ways of parenting to focusing on the best interests of their children.

We need to stop right here, because I know what you are thinking. You and your ex can't agree on anything. Even simple things become big between you. You think she is inflexible. He thinks you are stubborn. You wonder how I can be so positive that you and your ex will be able to effectively plan for your children. It takes two to plan, after all. How in the world will you be able to not only agree, but work on a plan together?

The answer is that you really do agree on some things. The problem is in how you both think about what you want for your children. Consider this: most of the time, you have a position about something. "I know what is right for our children" is a position. When you think of it this way, one person is right . . .

and the other person is wrong. But, if you work from the idea that you and your ex *share common interests*, right and wrong fade into the background.

Common interests are basic ideas of what you both want for your children. Here are some examples:

- We agree that our children should be healthy.
- We agree that our children should obey the law.
- We agree that our children should have a good education.

From these common interests, you can build a plan that leads to the goals connected to each interest. "We agree that our children should be healthy" becomes "Yearly checkups at the doctor, dentist, and eye doctor" in the parenting plan. I am not saying that it is easy or a quick fix. You would not be reading this book if it were easy. But it is possible. What's more, it's probable, if you keep your children as the focus.

In the second phase of parenting coordination, parents learn skills to set and maintain boundaries. One example of a boundary is changing how you interact with your coparent. During and after the divorce, parents stop being lovers or companions and learn to start acting like they are in a cordial, business-type relationship. Setting this type of boundary allows you to keep the children as a focus—even when provoked. Even when the other parent fails or forgets. Even when the other parent says something hurtful or rude. Boundaries keep small things from becoming huge. They can keep a random remark ("You're unreliable") from becoming another battle. Boundaries also keep conflict away from the children. As we will read in the next section, conflict is the most damaging part of any divorce.

TRY THIS:

The next time you need to talk about changing plans, such as weekend care, say "I" instead of "you." Say, for example, "I would really like it if you would think about swapping next weekend with me" instead of "You are never flexible."

This second phase also teaches effective ways to talk with your children. Divorce can lead to bad communication habits between children and parents. Children may be afraid of taking sides, or they may learn to play one parent against another to get what they want. Parents may get in the habit of talking down about their ex to the children. Good communication needs to be in place even when your children make you angry (or sad, or guilty). Children, just like adults, can push our buttons. Learning to stick to healthy ways of communication keeps everyone on track—you and the children.

The last phase of parenting coordination is maintenance. The plan may need to be "recalculated" due to a missed or wrong turn. Or you may get remarried, changing the way the family looks again. The parenting plan will be adjusted and the destination checked to be sure that you and your children are on track.

Parenting coordination works. A study in 2010, called the Parenting Coordination Project, found that, after six months in the program, parents reported much less hostility and anger with one another and a significant improvement in their ability to work together cooperatively. This study also found that children were much less anxious and stressed after their parents had been working with a Parenting Coordinator.

Several other studies (Fieldstone et al. 2012; Hayes et al. 2012; Henry et al. 2009) found that, after working with a parenting coordinator for one year, parents filed fewer legal motions and were able to resolve almost all of their child-related disputes without having to go back to court. Compared with families who only went to court, parents who worked with a Parenting Coordinator discussed problems together more often. The "nonresidential" parent (the parent who had the children for less of the time) participated more in the children's discipline than parents who did not use a parenting plan. These nonresidential parents were more active in the daily lives of their children, even though the children did not live with them full time. These parents helped with everyday things like helping the children get dressed, make science projects, and shop for birthday cards. They were also more active in special events, school and church functions, sports, holidays, and vacations.

It's Not Divorce That Hurts Children the Most—It's Conflict

Anger and conflict during divorce hurts children both now and later. It can affect how well they do in school and how they relate to friends now. Later in life, it can affect how they choose a wife or husband, and whether they can make a marriage last. Conflict during divorce shows up, for example, when parents can't agree on who gets the children for New Year's Day. The parents are angry, bitter, or show contempt for each other when talking about the holiday plans in front of the children. Or one parent has stricter rules at home than the other parent and fights with the other parent about the rules while the children listen. Children who see, hear, and feel this conflict will be hurt. It is not a question of *if* children will be hurt by conflict in a divorce, it's *how much* they will be hurt particularly when children are the focus or used to express the conflict.

Parent Behaviors That Put Children in the Middle:

- Asking children to carry hostile messages to the other parent
- Asking intrusive questions about the other parent
- Creating a need for children to hide information
- Creating a need for children to conceal their feelings about the other parent
- Demeaning or contemptuous of the other parent

This is not just my idea. Research proves that conflict between parents hurts children. A study by Dr. Irwin Sandler in 2013 showed that conflict between parents poses the greatest risk for harm to children—not the divorce itself. Even very young children notice conflict and will be harmed by it. The problem is, you won't see the harm right away. It looks like your children are doing okay. But they aren't fine. The conflict has left scars that may never heal. When I work with parents who don't want to change, I tell them, "It's your choice how many scars you will leave on the hearts of your children."

Another way to think of this harm is that it's like leaving a car running in the garage. The conflict between you and your ex is the running car. As long as the car is running, the poisonous fumes will seep into the garage. You can't see the fumes, but they are there, causing damage. As long as you leave the car running, your children will breathe the fumes. But if you take the car out of the garage and drive away, the children won't be near the fumes. You may still have to deal with the fumes, but you can deal with them away from the children. Another choice is turn the car off, open the garage door, and air out the garage. Either way works. You will protect your children. And that, after all, is your job as a parent.

You may be thinking that if your children have a good relationship with you, it will cancel out any bad feelings they might have from noticing the tension between you and your ex. Not true. A study conducted by Dr. Mavis Hetherington revealed that having good feelings for one parent can help alleviate only some of the stress the child feels about the conflict between parents. Children will still show negative effects from the hostility between parents. The longer the argument or conflict, the worse the effects are on children. What parents argue about doesn't matter. Children respond to the feeling of hostility, not to what is being said.

Mom and Dad fight all the time. He calls her bad names, and Mom yells at him. I hate going between their houses. I wish they would just STOP.

A researcher named Fabricius found that the amount of time spent at one parent's home or the others did not matter much in how children reacted to divorce. Even the "shape" of the caregiving network did not matter much—stepparents, relatives, and coparents could be almost any mix. The *important* factors in children adjusting to divorce are the parents' warmth, sensitivity, discipline style, and how well the parents work together. These factors will make the difference between a child who is well adjusted and a child who is scared, angry, and not doing well at home or at school.

There are a lot of studies about divorce because so many families are affected by divorce. According to Paul Amato, a professor of sociology at Pennsylvania State University, approximately one-half of all marriages in the United States end in divorce. The chance of a divorce in a second or third marriage is even higher. This means that literally millions of children are dealing with divorce in their family. The Kids Count Data Center (a project of the Annie E. Casey Foundation) reported that, in 2012, one-third (35 percent) of U.S. children under the age of eighteen were living with a single parent. Similar results were found in other regions around the globe (Americas, Europe, Oceania, and sub-Saharan Africa—World Family Map, 2014). In 2012 (Divorce Fact Sheet), the number of people in the "divorced" category in the United States was 145 million (46 percent), 27 million in the UK (43 percent), and 10 million in Australia (46 percent). In that same year, the annual number of divorces in Canada was 71,000 (43 percent).

As divorce has become a common experience for many families and we learn more about its effect on children, laws about divorce and children have changed. In the past, custody was usually given to the mother. Judges thought that mothers made the best parents for children. Today, custody or parental time-sharing is judged by the *best interests of the child.* The parent who might be "at fault" in a divorce will have as much right to parenting time with his or her children as the other parent. Some jurisdictions (courts within a particular geographic area) do not even talk about custody or visitation, but instead use terms like "parenting responsibilities" and "time-sharing" in divorce decisions. Instead of declaration of custody, there may be a *resident parent* and a *nonresident parent* where the resident parent has the child overnight more often than the other parent. In other areas, parents may have approximately equal amounts of time with their children and may simply be designated as parent A and parent B or the "on-duty" and "off-duty" parent in the parenting plan when referring to parenting time.

In this book I will not talk about custody. I will use the term "parenting plan." This covers not just times when a parent cares for the children in the home, but all the other things that go into parenting: health, school, faith, discipline, home rules, public rules, dress . . . the list goes on and on. These are just as important as where the child sleeps at night.

Changing the words used in divorce does not change the reality, however. Divorce may be the best move for parents, but it is hard for children. This is not to say that children in other eras never had to adjust to life with one parent or with one parent at a time. In the early 1900s, one quarter—25 percent—of children lost a parent to death before they were fifteen years old. Many of these children grew up in a one-parent home.

Divorce, though, is different from losing a parent through death. In a divorce the parents feel not just grief, but may also feel anger, blame, guilt, and regret. No one gets married thinking that the marriage will end in divorce. Many people see divorce as a failure, no matter who or what is to blame. This can lead to angry, confused feelings that get in the way of being a good parent. These feelings can show up unexpectedly and ambush you when you least expect it.

If you only had to think about yourself, having negative feelings after a divorce would be a problem, but you could handle it. But when children are involved, they can be hurt by the conflict they hear and see. A Canadian report on high-conflict divorce points out that what we as adults might call conflict won't necessarily be what a child interprets as conflict. Children may see conflict, for example, when a parent will not talk to the other parent while dropping them off. Refusing to open the door to the other parent is likely seen by children as conflict. Arguing and hitting between parents is obvious conflict, but so is the parent who makes a child carry a note to the other parent about late support payments.

> Robert Emery, PhD, has conducted and written over 100 studies and scientific papers on the effects of divorce on children. His research shows that divorce affects boys and girls differently. Boys will act out right away, with problems in school and at home. Girls often do not act out until they become teenagers. But both boys and girls of divorce are angrier than other children. They also are not as close to either parent as children whose parents have not divorced. The risk of adjustment problems is twice as high for children of divorce.

Children of divorce have many feelings about the divorce and their parents. You may see or hear these problems, or your children may keep them from you, not wanting to let you know how they are really feeling.

Loss
Children often have a sense of loss during and after a divorce. They may say or show you that they are sad. Some children will cry when they think about the changes in the family. Other children may have signs of depression: trouble sleeping, eating too much or too little, restlessness, and wandering attention.

Anxiety
Most children worry that their basic needs will not be

met. "Will we have enough money to live on now?" Many worry that they will be abandoned or left alone. They worry about their parents' emotional and physical health and not being able to see their friends.

Feeling rejected

Children often feel rejected by one or both parents. This can be real or imagined. "Dad doesn't want me." "If Mom really loved me, she would stay with Dad."

Loneliness

Children miss the parent who is not in the home. "I wish Mom were here." Children feel that they get less attention from both parents during divorce—not just one parent. It may even be true if money problems cause one or both parents to work longer hours after the divorce. Or one parent may move farther away, making time with that parent hard to arrange. Sometimes extended family members will try to be neutral in the divorce by not visiting either parent. This means the children are lonelier than ever, since aunts or uncles who used to visit are now staying away. The loss of their support can be hard for children.

Anger

Fear can lead to sadness or anger. Children can be afraid of being abandoned or just afraid of what they don't know. They may be angry with either parent—or with both parents.

Loyalty issues

Parents may compete for their children's affection and loyalty. One parent may take the children to amusement parks or buy them expensive toys, while the other cannot afford the money or time to match what the other parent is doing. Children walk a tightrope, afraid that fun and closeness with one parent might be a betrayal of the other parent.

The Justice Department of Canada studies children of divorce on an ongoing basis. These studies highlight problems of children in families of divorce. Poor grades in school are often seen in these studies (Grych & Fincham, 1992; Brody & Neubaum, 1996). Poor grades can be due to not paying attention and lack of interest in school because the child is depressed. Behavior problems can crop up when the child is angry. Fighting, name-calling, and picking fights can be a problem at school or at home. Sometimes the behavior problems lead to a run-in with the police.

Behavior problems, what psychologists call "acting out," were seen in the Canadian studies not only in violent behavior, but also in sexuality. Many teenagers of divorce started having sex early. This can lead to pregnancy and sexually transmitted diseases, which will affect the rest of their lives. Acting out is also seen in a negative attitude toward one or both parents. Children often left home earlier than they had planned, sometimes before finishing high school.

Some children turn inward instead of acting out. These children show a fear of abandonment ("I will be left alone with nobody to take care of me"). Some children drop out of social

CRANBERRY PUBLIC LIBRARY
2525 ROCHESTER ROAD, SUITE 300
CRANBERRY TOWNSHIP, PA 16066
724-776-9100

groups like soccer teams or church groups. Another reaction is to develop negative ideas about romance and marriage ("I won't get married until I find the perfect woman. Look what happened with Mom and Dad"). Some children will show several of these problems, while some might only show one or two. Every child reacts differently to divorce.

Judith Wallerstein was one of the first psychologists to study families after divorce. She spoke with over a hundred parents and children to understand how the divorce affected them. Her study went on for twenty-five years, in order to determine the long-term effects of divorce. She found that a third of children were still caught in their parents' bitterness five years after the divorce. Knowing the negative effects of conflict on children, this is a warning bell for parents who divorce. If you are in the third of bitterly divorced parents, the findings from scientific studies can help you to make a decision vital to your children's well-being. You can decide to shield your children from the conflict that can harm them. You can decide to focus on your children. It's a good investment for both you and your children.

Your Parenting Style Counts

Your "style" of parenting makes a big difference in how well your children will cope with your divorce. As we talked about earlier, studies have shown that how well you get along with the other parent is important. So is the warmth and sensitivity you show to your children. Being a warm parent does not mean that you are lax with rules. You can be very strict and still be a warm parent. In this case, warmth is how you show your children you care about them: hugs, smiles, and saying positive things around them.

Sensitivity is basically paying attention. This means listening and focusing on what your children say, and what they do not say out loud. It can be hard to pay attention when there is so much to do and so little time to do it in. Children can chatter on about what seems to be nothing at all. The chatter is a way to get your attention. You may be distracted by a long "to do" list. Picking your children up to take them to soccer practice is just one more thing on your list. Those fifteen minutes in the car, however, is their time to make a connection to you. Pay attention. Let the children know you are focused on them—smile, nod, or comment on what they are talking about. Notice if they are slumping in the seat or looking sad. Ask about what is going on. Your involvement in these little moments is one of the keys to positive parenting.

Judith Cashmore, a law professor, has researched the effects of day-to-day involvement in their children's lives by parents who are divorced. One study looked at overnight stays of children with the nonresident parent (remember, that is the parent who has the children for less time than the other parent). Keeping children overnight, with the routines of getting them ready for bed, making and keeping rules, and offering them comfort, has a very positive effect on the children *and* the overnight parent. The overnight parent, who is often the father, becomes more comfortable providing care that the children's mother would normally give. The children feel closer and have a better relationship with the overnight parent.

The overnight parents told the researchers that when they first started taking the children overnight, it was a little uncomfortable. Would they do the right things? What if something went wrong? But the overnight parents learned what worked best with their children. Soon they were confident in their skills as parents. The overnight visits became satisfying to both the parents and the children.

Even very young children benefit from overnight visits. Marsha Kline Pruett and colleagues (2014) looked at how babies develop different skills based on parenting by mom and parenting by dad. These studies showed that when fathers are involved in their babies' lives, the babies develop better skills as they grow up compared to babies who rarely see their fathers. Mothers are not the only ones who can care for very young children. Dads can be great parents—even to infants and toddlers.

Our Family Redefined

Divorce is not something that happens once in a courtroom. It is a *lifetime* change for you and your family. The family looks different now. Old patterns have to be changed. New patterns have to be tried out and then kept or thrown away. In some areas, there is a mandatory waiting period before a couple can divorce. This can be good or bad. When divorce takes longer to finalize and parents are able to work together, the family has time to gradually figure out how the new family will look and act. Parents can try out different plans and see what works and what doesn't work. Children have time to get used to the idea that their family is going to look different. But, if parents are not working together, the children stay caught in the middle of the conflict for a much longer time and are at greater risk for *never* adjusting well after the divorce.

Separation can happen literally overnight. Dad (or Mom) moves out and doesn't come back. Many states and provinces with no-fault divorce can process the legal divorce in very little time. Children and parents suddenly need to make changes in almost every area of life. It seems as if every minute there is one more detail to sort out. The stress level for everyone stays high because there is no rest period in comfortable routines.

Sudden change in families is not unique to divorce, however. It is a normal process that happens in other circumstances as well: with a move to another town due to a job change, a new baby born into the family, or the death of a family member. Routines are shaken up and for a while it feels as if things will never be easy again. But, gradually, new routines take shape. You find new ways to cope, as individuals and as a family. You help one another to figure out what the family will look like now. The family has been redefined—just as a word is redefined when it is suddenly used in new and different ways. This new family moves ahead with different ways to cope with its current reality.

You have a new role now: "coparent." As a coparent, you are responsible for working with the other parent to care for your children. Together, you get parenting tasks done. You set up dentist appointments, arrange for dance lessons, and plan for sports. You give your children a sense of common purpose. Your ex is now essentially your business partner and your business mission is this: "Working together for our children".

Karen and Carl were still very angry with one another two years after their divorce. They had many conflicts and had been back in court many times. During a recent court visit, Karen accused Carl of putting Carl Junior in danger by letting him walk to the grocery store by himself. Carl, in turn, asked the court not to let Carl Junior visit Karen because she had a live-in boyfriend who Carl thought was a bad influence. When Carl had come to pick Carl Junior up for his regular Wednesday parenting time, Karen locked the door and screamed at Carl that she would not let their son go with him until he promised not to let Carl Junior walk to the store alone. Carl called Karen a "f----- b----" and threatened that he would "take Carl Junior away forever." Carl Junior, a second grader, has begun to pick fights at school. His grades have dropped and he has lost weight. The court ordered Carl and Karen to meet with a Parenting Coordinator. The Parenting Coordinator worked with Karen and Carl to help them focus on Carl Junior's best interests: safety, health, and a good education. Karen and Carl began to learn how to shift their focus from themselves as the "angry ex-couple" to "Carl Junior's parents." The Parenting Coordinator taught them about the developmental stages of children—what is normal for a child Carl Junior's age—so they could decide together whether walking to the store alone was okay for a boy his age. Additionally, Carl Junior began receiving counseling from a therapist skilled in working with children of divorce.

It was not an easy process, because Karen and Carl had been fighting almost nonstop for more than two years. But when they were able to separate their angry feelings for each other from parenting issues, things began to move quickly. The Parenting Coordinator helped them develop a parenting plan that gave them a road map for parenting Carl Junior. The road map keeps conflict out of Carl Junior's sight by laying out the direction for parenting time, rules for Carl Junior, and rules for each other.

Carl Junior's grades improved and he made the traveling soccer team the next year. "I'm glad that my parents aren't fighting so much," says Carl Junior. "Now I don't feel bad about wanting to be with Daddy. I don't have to take sides."

Research shows that parenting plans work. If you and your coparent agree on (1) what is best for your children, and (2) have a clear plan for parenting roles and responsibilities, and (3) keep to the plan, conflict can be managed and children spared from its negative effects. If you are interested in looking into these studies and others mentioned in this chapter, or would like to look into other research, see chapter 9.

Using research as a foundation for parenting will keep you focused on what works. This is the practical approach used in a parenting plan. Although "flying by the seat of your pants" can work, it's stressful and has a high rate of crash and burn. A parenting plan that uses proven techniques is less likely to fail—and it's less stressful. Follow the plan and you should arrive at the destination on time and in one piece.

CHAPTER TWO

Satellites

GPS units use satellites that send and receive information so you can tell not only where you are, but *when* you are there. GPS systems contain a clock that keeps track of time no matter where you are. The GPS signals come in from over thirty satellites. The satellites travel around the earth at different angles to get the best coverage of the earth below. At any one time, ten or more satellites can "see" the GPS unit. Then the satellite's orbit takes it behind the earth for a while, until its orbit brings it back into sight. In this way the GPS can track both location and time.

The GPS parenting plan works in much the same way. The "satellites" in this case are the many factors that need to be tracked to ensure your children stay on course. What are these factors? Physical health, mental health, and education are what most parents think of when planning for their children's well-being. But social factors are important too—friends, grandparents, aunts and uncles, and the rest of *both* families. What if the parenting plan did not include regular visits with Grandma? Both your children and their grandmother would miss out. Religion is also an important social factor for many families. All of these things need to be part of the parenting plan.

The parenting plan also accounts for the changes that occur with time. As time passes, your children get older. They change as they grow. Their needs change too. The plan for a toddler will look different from a plan for a teenager. Building in changes that allow for the normal development of children will make the plan work over time, as the journey of childhood goes by. Later in this chapter we will examine the normal stages of childhood in detail.

The Parenting Coordinator works with you to incorporate all of the important factors for your children in the parenting plan. As you might expect, Parenting Coordinators have training and experience in family law. They are also trained in parenting education, case management, mental health, child development, and community resources. Their background in knowing what children might need as they grow allows Parenting Coordinators to refer children to the services they need.

The Parenting Coordinator acts like the resources button on the GPS. Press this button to find fuel, food, services, and points of interest. The Parenting Coordinator might see that tutoring is needed to help resolve a child's problem in school. Or counseling is needed for a child who is acting out. Tutoring and counseling resources are then plugged into the parenting plan.

The GPS maps out the directions and distance to the resource you need. The Parenting Coordinator has resources close at hand, just like the GPS. Parents are spared the problem of not knowing which way to turn when a bump in the road causes a problem. For example, the Parenting Coordinator may give you information about how children behave at different ages. The Parenting Coordinator would not, however, personally counsel your children when they have problems as teenagers but would refer them to a therapist. Think of it this way: the GPS in your car can find Kentucky Fried Chicken for you ... but the GPS doesn't serve lunch.

This is Not Fair

You have probably felt misunderstood, helpless, unfairly treated, and trapped in the court system during the divorce process. Sometimes it feels as if the system adds to your problems instead of eliminating them. Courts can be slow, complicated, and expensive. The legal system can also feel like there is an "us-versus-them" way of looking at divorce. The system is set up so most parents feel like they are either a "winner" or a "loser," and often both parents feel like they lost. There doesn't seem to be any way for everyone to win, even just some of the time.

However, the Parenting Coordinator, working as the GPS, is keeping track of your children for the court. When I work with families in this way, I am the eyes and ears of the court. This keeps families out of court—and out of the win/lose court process. It doesn't make sense for parents to go to court to resolve simple issues, such as whether the pickup for children should be at the local gas station or the grocery store. That is a parenting decision, not a court decision. My goal is to keep the courts clear for legal issues.

This is not just about avoiding court, although that can be cheaper and easier for you. I also want to offer you a dose of hope. Right now you may have lost any hope that things can get better. It feels as if you and your coparent are stuck. She will never get over being angry. He will never listen. But after twenty-five years of working with parents just like you, I would like to tell you that things *can* change. I have seen it happen again and again. It is not easy. There is a lot of learning to do. You will have habits to break. You will need to learn new ways to communicate. But the skills and tools you learn will help you for the rest of your life. Best of all, what you learn will give your children a better life.

Getting Started

There is not a "one-size-fits-all" Parenting Coordinator. Your Parenting Coordinator may be a psychologist, a social worker, a mediator, or an attorney. He may work under strict local laws, or be hired privately by you without a court order. He may have a warm style or may be very straightforward with you. All Parenting Coordinators have a common goal, though, and will base their work on scientific studies. This "evidence-based practice" means that the Parenting Coordinator is not guessing about what will work best for your children. He knows. He has read the research and keeps up with the latest findings.

Parenting coordination begins with information. What is the family like? What do you as coparents see as needs? What can you agree on as the best interests of your children? Many Parenting Coordinators will give you homework—forms to fill out with information to start the process. I have included some of these forms here and in later chapters for your use. They include information forms and self-assessment forms to identify your parenting style.

The following is a questionnaire to help you determine if parenting coordination would be helpful in your case. It's also available as a form called the ***Screening Questionnaire for Parent Coordination Services*** on The National Cooperative Parenting Center (NCPC) website here: www.TheNCPC.com.

1. Please rate your current relationship with your child(ren)'s other parent (coparent). Check one:

☐ Hostile/Frightening
☐ Bitter/Angry
☐ Distant/Cold
☐ Polite/Respectful
☐ Friendly

2. Please check all the issues, events, or situations that cause problems for you and your coparent:

☐ Who pays for what
☐ Putting children's needs first
☐ Pick-up/drop-off time
☐ Making decisions about school
☐ Different standards (what grades kids should get, what friends they should have, etc.)
☐ Buying kids things they need
☐ Buying gifts for kids
☐ Discipline
☐ Vacation time
☐ Curfew (how late kids can stay up on school nights or weekends)
☐ Stepparent or live-in lover
☐ School performance
☐ Wanting more flexibility
☐ Last-minute changes in schedule
☐ Wanting more structure
☐ Relationships with in-laws
☐ Attendance at school functions (conferences, plays, games, etc.)
☐ Grandparents' involvement with kids

☐ Your ex's personal habits (cursing, drinking, smoking, etc.)
☐ Religious differences
☐ How to handle emergencies
☐ Different ideas about getting medical treatment for kids
☐ Division of parenting time
☐ Things that bothered you when you were married
☐ Your ex's dating habits
☐ Different ideas about diet and exercise for kids

3. I respect the mother/father of my child(ren) as a parent:
☐ Never
☐ Rarely
☐ Sometimes
☐ Usually
☐ Always

4. If I don't agree with my coparent's approach to child-rearing, I can accept that we are different and still support him or her:
☐ Never
☐ Rarely
☐ Sometimes
☐ Usually
☐ Always

5. I keep myself from talking badly about my coparent in front of the child(ren):
☐ Never
☐ Rarely
☐ Sometimes
☐ Usually
☐ Always

6. I believe my coparent does not speak badly about me in front of the child(ren):

☐ Never
☐ Rarely
☐ Sometimes
☐ Usually
☐ Always

7. I discuss with my coparent issues that are important to the child(ren), such as health, school, sports, family events, and awards:

☐ Never
☐ Rarely
☐ Sometimes
☐ Usually
☐ Always

8. My coparent is willing to discuss with me any important issues about our child(ren):

☐ Never
☐ Rarely
☐ Sometimes
☐ Usually
☐ Always

9. I think it is important for my child(ren) to maintain regular contact with his or her other parent and family (grandparents, aunts, uncles, cousins) no matter what I think of them:

☐ Never
☐ Rarely
☐ Sometimes

☐ Usually
☐ Always

10. I believe my coparent feels it is important for my child(ren) to keep regular contact with me and my family no matter what she or he thinks of us:

☐ Never
☐ Rarely
☐ Sometimes
☐ Usually
☐ Always

SCORING

Item 1: If either of the first two choices are marked (Hostile/Frightening or Bitter/Angry), parenting coordination services are recommended.

Item 2: If eight or more items are checked, parenting coordination services are recommended.

Items 5–10: If never, rarely, or sometimes is checked, parenting coordination services are recommended.

© *2009 Debra K. Carter, National Cooperative Parenting Center*

The information about your family can be used for what is called a SWOT analysis of the family. In business management, the SWOT analysis looks at strengths, weaknesses, opportunities, and threats. What are the *strengths* of the parents and the family system? Are there *weaknesses* that need to be addressed? What *opportunities* are there for this family? And lastly, what are the risk factors for parents and children—*threats* to the children's well-being?

Strengths

It is not as easy as you might think to list the strengths in your family. During a divorce, it is too easy to only see the negative. You may be so angry with your coparent that it is hard to think of one good thing about her. "She packs a good lunch for the kids" may be the best you can come up with at first. *Focusing on the children helps make this clearer.* The reason you got a divorce was not because she is a bad parent. Problems in the "wife" area led to the divorce, not problems with her parenting skills. Think about your coparent as she is with your children. Is she good at managing school schedules? Does she encourage the children to be active in sports and school? Is she calm when there is a medical emergency? All of these are strengths.

Seeing only the negative can happen with either coparent. Many moms think that only a woman can be a good parent. Our culture has often seen men as second-class parents. As I mentioned earlier, scientific studies have proven this is not true. Men can be just as good at parenting as women.

There are many basics in your family that can be counted as strengths: a steady job, a low mortgage payment, health insurance, and a flexible work schedule. A supportive church, synagogue, or mosque can also be a positive for the family. Grandparents who can help with child care can be a big help to the family, especially if the grandparents are positive and shelter the children from conflict. A grandparent who is critical and demeaning of one or both parents can cause the same problems as conflict between parents. Fumes are fumes, whether they are given off by parents or grandparents.

Weaknesses

Family strengths can also be their weaknesses. A church may be supportive when you are married, but have harsh rules about divorce. The support may vanish after you are divorced. Or your coparent may remarry someone of another faith. Conflict may come up about what faith the children should be raised in.

A steady job can be a positive unless the work hours don't allow you to take the children to doctor's appointments. Other weaknesses might include health issues with your coparent. As long as she takes her medication, she is fine. But the medication may make her too tired at times to pick up the children. This is a known weakness that can be factored into the parenting plan.

Another possible weakness is parenting style. Your coparent may have a completely different way of setting rules for your children than you do. Conflict may come up because your rules don't match. This is *not* always a weakness. Sometimes different styles of parenting lead to the same end, even though they are different. "At Mom's house we eat two veggies at dinner. Dad gives us fruit or a tomato drink, since he is not such a good cook."

Opportunities

Sometimes opportunities open up unexpectedly. An after-school program may start a special program for kids of divorced parents. A piano teacher may move in next door. Your job may give you a chance to work from home two days a week, making after-school care easier. Opportunities will come and go. Recognize them as they arise in order to use them for your children's good.

Threats

Threats in the family can be risks—things that *might* happen—or actual problems happening right now. Your ex might be a recovering alcoholic. The risk would be if he fell off the wagon and started drinking again. It's not happening now, but it is a risk nonetheless. An actual threat to the family might be money problems that make it hard to sustain two households. Another kind of threat is an emergency threat. This is a threat that can cause immediate harm to anyone in the family. *Violence in the family is an emergency.* I will talk about this in depth later, but for now, if you or anyone in the family is in danger from violence, flip to chapter 7 for the number to a domestic violence hotline. It's that important. Don't wait.

Knowing strengths, weaknesses, opportunities, and threats makes the parenting plan more likely to succeed. Some problems can be prevented before they happen in the first place. But if problems do arise, the Parenting Coordinator can be the calm problem-solver in the middle of the crisis. As a parent, you can be too close to the problem. You may be so close, in fact, that it is hard to see past how urgent the problem feels. It can be easy to overlook what is really important—not just urgent.

Problem-solving also means looking for patterns: Has this happened before? Have the children gone off track in just this same way? How do we keep this from happening again? The "why" of what went wrong is often even more important than what went wrong. Keeping the big picture in mind and looking for patterns is a critical part of the parenting plan.

The Parenting Coordinator is also your resource for legal information. He will know the laws in your state or province about divorce, parenting time, and parenting plans. He will know how to communicate with the court and can save you time (and money) in the court system. This person can also interpret court orders into plain English. What's more, he will know when it is important for you to speak to an attorney about your rights and the impact of decisions you make about parenting issues. The Parenting Coordinator will not provide legal advice, but can help you identify the best way to get the advice you need.

Navigating a New Parenting Journey

Change can be frightening, especially when something as valuable as your children are concerned. Most people hesitate to start a journey without knowing where they are going, how to get there, or the roadblocks they may encounter along the way. Learning to coparent after separation and divorce is a new journey for most people. It is also one that most are not prepared to take. If your own parents stayed married throughout your childhood, there are no role models for how to carry on after a divorce. Or if your parents divorced but it was a painful time, the healthy role models may not be there either. "I won't do that to my children," you might say to yourself. You have a model of what not to do, but not of what you should do.

The Guidance for Parenting System gives parents, children, and families a road map for the journey. Parents develop and maintain a new way to work with each other and their children to deal with all the changes taking place in the family system. GPS offers a chance for all family members to find new ways of thinking, feeling, and acting. A plan gives everyone a sense of security. You aren't walking in a minefield anymore. You have a map that tells you the safe way to go.

Maintenance

Every system needs to receive a steady supply of energy or it will quit working. A GPS is the same. Whether it is from a battery or power from the car, the GPS requires energy to operate. Your family is no different. It, too, is a system that needs power to keep working. In this case, the power is the energy put into caring for your children. Who supplies this energy? You, your coparent, and a Parenting Coordinator. Others put energy into the system as well—perhaps grandparents, teachers, your rabbi, the Girl Scout leader, friends, and counselors. You will all keep putting energy into the system until your children are adults.

Systems not only need energy; they also require maintenance. Nothing works forever without needing repairs or tune-ups. For example, once a year each GPS satellite must fire its engines to push it back into the proper orbit. Gravity pulls the satellite toward the earth, and this changes its orbit slightly. Without the yearly push from the engines, the satellite's orbit would continue to veer off course. Trying to fix the orbit now takes a long burn from the engines to produce enough power to boost it back into the right orbit. If this isn't done, the satellite will eventually fall so low that it reaches the point of no return. Then it will start to burn as it speeds toward the ground— flames shooting out as it moves across the sky—and crashes into the earth or falls into the sea. Parts of the satellite might be found and repaired. Other times, however, it crashes into the hard ground in a million pieces.

The Earth's pull on satellites can be compared to old habits and behaviors that pull you and your children off course. It is easy to slip back into unhelpful behavior, especially when the new way of doing things hasn't become a habit yet. It is also easy to coast along, not putting energy into the family system. The effects aren't seen at first. You can coast for a while without problems. You don't pay attention. But you are slowing down. At this point, problems will soon pop up. Only now it takes twice as much energy to get the plan back on track. You can eventually reach the point where the problems are so hard to fix that your plan crashes and burns. Maintenance is much easier, in the long run, than repair.

Your parenting plan needs your attention and energy over time. When you begin to create a plan, there is a lot to do. There are forms to fill out and meetings to attend. You will have homework—reading, calling the children's schools for documents, or checking on dental records. Then you will be busy with the nuts and bolts of the plan: determining the best interests of your children, discovering areas where you and your coparent don't agree, identifying team members to bring into the plan, and finally, writing the plan itself.

Once the plan is established, energy is still needed, but not as much or as often. A maintenance schedule is set up. You will keep checking on the plan just as you would glance at the GPS when driving to be sure you are still on course. On track? Check. Speed limit? Check. Gas levels? Check. Now you can focus on enjoying the journey.

Waypoints: Developmental Stages

Waypoints are used on a GPS to mark locations along the way to the final destination. They can be entered by users ("Grandma's house") or downloaded from the GPS ("Jonesboro State Park"). Waypoints not only tell you how far you have come; they often serve a safety purpose as well. You can set up waypoints to route yourself around known road hazards.

In parenting, developmental stages serve as waypoints. Children normally change every few years. Studies of the way children change, and how long it takes them to reach specific milestones, give us a pretty good idea of what is normal for children of a certain age, and what is not. Known hazards are laid out so you can avoid them—or at least be aware of them. Yet it's impossible to avoid some hazards. They are part of growing up, and your children are going to encounter them no matter what you do. But knowing about them can help you and your children cope. Consider this dad's experience:

> *As a single dad, I thought I knew how to be a parent. Things went fine for a while. But then nothing I did seemed to work. All of a sudden, I was the worst dad in history. After reading about developmental stages in children, I found out that my daughter had moved into a new stage. There was a really good reason why nothing was working. It wasn't me; it was my daughter's age. I switched some of my dad rules, and things evened out. I'm waiting for the next stage, but now I know what's coming up next. I won't be surprised this time.*

Birth to Eighteen Months: Bonding and Learning to Trust

A parenting plan is needed for babies as well as older children. In fact, the early years are so important that this is probably the most critical time to have a solid parenting plan.

Points to Remember in a Parenting Plan for an Infant

- Frequent, repeated contact with each parent is best.
- Contact should provide time for feeding, playing,

bathing, soothing, napping, and nighttime sleeping.

- Both parents must develop the skills to be good caregivers.

- Infants should not be away from either parent for more than a few days, if possible.

- Parents need to share their experiences in order to provide consistency and stability for child care. They must do this in a way that does not expose the child to anger and that is comforting to the infant.

Learning to trust other people is one of the first—and most important—social skills we learn as children. The first two years of life are a critical time for your children to learn trust. Babies form trusting bonds with the important people around them. How these bonds are formed depends on the amount of time and the quality of the care given to the baby. It does not matter whether the person giving care is male or female. Moms, dads, grandmothers, or grandfathers can teach babies to trust. Learning to trust others is an important skill that your child will use in the years to come with friends, teachers, and other family members. Later in life it will make the difference between a good marriage and a bad one. Trust is the foundation for dealing with other people.

For a baby, trust means that her needs will be met. If a baby is hungry, she cries. Someone comes when she cries and gives her food. Knowing that this will happen gives her trust in others. It has to happen right away, though. Babies are not able to "see" you when you are out of sight. Their brains cannot hold a picture of you as comfort. A baby can't think, "Mom will be here in ten minutes. Just wait." Everything for a baby is *now*. This means that babies require a lot of their caretakers' time. That time has to be "just in time" too—which means you need to be available for whatever the child needs, right away. It also means that short time-sharing plans are a must. Consider what happened in this case:

The parents of a nine-month-old child had a time-sharing plan set up by the court for a change between the mom and dad every other week. When the plan was implemented, the child soon had trouble sleeping and wouldn't eat regularly. Initially, each parent was blaming the other. When the couple came to see me for parenting coordination, it was clear that both parents cared a great deal for their child. The child's problems had nothing to do with their parenting. It was the schedule that was the problem. Every week their baby went through fear and anxiety as the primary caregiver changed. The baby was not old enough to remember that Mom (or Dad) would come back. It was a trauma every week.

We changed the time-sharing plan so that each parent had parenting time with the baby every day, and grandma agreed to pick up the child at each handover so the baby would also bond with the grandmother. We monitored the baby's adjustment for several months to see if these changes were helping. Eventually, the baby's eating and sleeping problems disappeared and the baby began to thrive. We were then able to develop a time-sharing plan that required fewer exchanges between the parents because the baby was older and able to tolerate a little more time away from each parent without experiencing trauma and loss.

During their child's first eighteen months of life, parents should do the following:

- Spend time holding and cuddling the child.
- Provide for the child's basic needs right away.
- Keep the child on a regular schedule (for sleeping, eating, playing, and so on).
- Keep up with regular doctor's appointments (well-baby checkups).
- Keep conflict away from the child.

Another road hazard in this stage is stranger anxiety. This happens between five and ten months of age. Although developing anxiety around strangers or people who are not the child's primary caregivers is a normal part of development, it doesn't look that way. Suddenly a happy child cries and gets very upset when leaving one parent for the other. Coparents may suspect that the other parent is abusing the child: "Look how scared Pamela is of you! Are you hurting her?" The answer is that Pamela may not recognize the other parent in different clothes or with a new haircut. Or several weeks have passed, and Pamela will need some time to remember the coparent. It is a good idea to go slow during this stage of stranger anxiety. Don't hand off the child quickly. Give her time to warm up to the coparent (or grandmother, or babysitter). Speak in a low, calm voice. Have the coparent offer the child a favorite toy. Let the child smell the coparent's clothes and see his face. Take your time, and the child will relax.

At this age, children can sense tension and conflict between their parents. Children won't be able to understand why there might be conflict, but they know it is there. If parents are anxious and angry, children will react and may be colicky and difficult to soothe. Watch out for these problems in children at this age, as they may be a sign that your children are breathing the fumes:

- Experiencing delays in development—well-baby checkups will keep track of this
- Acting fussy when parents are upset
- Not gaining enough weight, not growing well
- Not responding to you; seems listless and tired all the time
- Appearing fretful or nervous

Remember: Same Routine, Difference Parent and Place

- Each parent should follow the same daily routines, including feeding, bathing, putting the child down to sleep, and waking the child up from a nap. This will help the child develop a secure relationship and help both parents master the tasks of caretaking.

- Avoid separations of more than three days, as these may interfere with the child's sense of safety and stability. Strive to balance work responsibilities with the child's need for regular involvement with each parent during the weekdays and shared time on weekends.

- Each household should follow similar patterns and routines in child care to provide consistency.

Eighteen Months to Three Years: Personality Development

This is the age when you really notice that your child is unique. He is becoming his own person, even at this young age. He now begins to play with other children. At first this play is more to get the attention of adults. Later, play is more side-by-side play with other children.

The "terrible twos" happen during this stage. Your happy child, who was pleased just to be with you, now is not pleased with anything. "No" is her favorite word. She is demanding. She wants that toy and only that toy. She won't eat when you want her to. Life seems to be a struggle for control. And it is. Your child is learning to act on her own. Parents with children in this stage should do the following:

- Follow routines. Schedules are comforting to the child, even if the child says "no."
- Tell *and* show your child that you love him. Hugs, pats, and kisses are important at this age.
- Set limits. Rules are comforting. The child needs to hear "no"—and hear it every time. Don't say "no" five times and then say "yes." Doing so will create an even more demanding child. Be firm. Be consistent. Be loving while being firm and consistent.
- Keep up with regular doctor's appointments. Keep a journal of any problems so you can let the doctor know what has been going on. For example, "Last month Parker started sucking his thumb again."

At this age, children need to know that they will be cared for by parents and others. Rather than just saying "I love you," show it with actions. Hugs are important, but so are rules and boundaries. Knowing where the "do not cross" lines are helps your child know that he is cared for and safe. Don't be afraid to be a parent: set rules and stick by them.

Children this age will notice conflict between their parents. Conflict will make children afraid and nervous. They may not have very many words in their vocabulary yet, and are not likely to have words to express their feelings, such as why they are afraid. At this age, naming feelings is still being learned. You may see thumb-sucking or other "younger" behaviors crop back up in children who had stopped this behavior.

Watch out for these problems in children at this age, as they may be caused by conflict between parents:

- Frequent "accidents" after being out of diapers for many months
- Thumb sucking
- Fearfulness
- Withdrawal or moodiness
- Demanding more attention than usual or tantrums
- Changes in sleeping and eating

Tips for Parenting Toddlers

- Transitions can be difficult unless both parents have soothing styles and can meet the child's needs for structure and reassurance.

- Adjust your parenting to meet the child's need for success. When coparents use similar ways of handling events, it provides a sense of comfort to the child.

- Use telephone or webcam calls at a regular hour for the child and the "away" parent to touch base. This keeps the relationship in the present.

- Place a picture of each parent in the child's room along with the "special blanket or teddy" that travels back and forth between the homes. This can be reassuring to the child.

- Speak positively about the "away" parent. This reassures the child of the other parent's return and helps keep the "away" parent present.

- Space overnights throughout the week.

Three Years to Five Years: Different Ways of Thinking

Children at this age are learning to think for themselves. They can seem older than they are when talking. One five-year-old said to his mother, "I think you left your cell phone in Dad's car. That is my hypothesis." Amazed at her son's vocabulary, his mother asked him what "hypothesis" meant. "It's an idea about what happened, of course," the boy said.

Parents should be careful not to think that their children are emotionally as old as they may sound. Preschoolers often confuse reality with fantasy. They may believe that dreams can still come true, as well as thoughts, feelings, and wishes. This can be a problem if the child thinks that he can make the divorce "not happen" by wishing or by behaving in a certain way. Confused thinking may make the child feel that it was his misbehavior that caused the divorce.

At this age, children get their feeling of security from the environment that surrounds them. If the home is stable and secure, they will feel safe. It is hard for children to understand that conflict at home is not their fault or that it will ever end. Feelings are "now" for preschool children. Parents with children in this stage should do the following:

- Show and tell your child that you love her.
- Tell your child several times that your coparent will come back. "Mom is coming for you in two days. Let's look at the calendar and count."
- Read child-level books on divorce with your child. See chapter 9 for recommended books.
- Even though your child may use grown-up words, use simple language with her to explain the divorce. Repeat it often.

- Help your child talk about how he feels. You may need to label feelings for him. "Are you sad, Parker? Or are you mad?"
- Ask your child if she is having scary dreams or other scary thoughts.
- Keep up with regular doctor's appointments.

Watch out for these issues in children at this age, which may be related to the divorce:

- Wishful thinking. "You and Mommy are getting back together, right?"
- Tantrums, thumb-sucking, or bedwetting
- Fears about things other than divorce; a general fearful manner
- Trying to control what happens ("We're doing *this* now!")
- Worry that Mom or Dad will never come back

A special word to parents of children who are five years or younger: stay involved. It might be easier to drift out of your children's lives if it seems like you and your coparent are at constant war or the children resist coming to stay with you. Children are a lot of work when they are so young. Parenting can be really hard now. If you child clings to your coparent or cries when you reach to get her, you may feel like a failure and very hurt. But . . . hang in there. Research shows that you—both of you, Mom and Dad—are vitally important now. These are the years when your children set the foundation for the rest of their lives. You can't make up for lost time later. Your time to be involved is now. Keep being a parent. It will be worth it.

Tips for Parenting Preschool and Early Kindergarten Children

- Take your child's temperament into consideration.

- Each parent should be comfortable in helping the child with the daily routine, including getting ready for the new experience of school.

- Both parents should participate in the daily routines like feeding, playing, bathing, and reading.

- Encourage your child to take on some responsibility for self-care (such as picking up toys, flushing the toilet, and washing hands before meals) to develop independence and responsibility.

- If both parents were involved in all aspects of care (before the separation), the child may be able to be away from either parent for two or three days without becoming distressed. This may depend on the child's temperament.

Five Years to Eleven Years: The Need for Family and Belonging

During this stage, children use the family as an anchor. Family keeps them safe in one place while they explore the world. Divorce can be very hard for children this age to accept. Most school-age children believe that their parents will get back together. This belief can result from the smallest of cues— Mom inviting Dad to attend the child's birthday party, or Dad suggesting that everyone go for ice cream after the baseball game. Often, children will blow up these small acts to mean that Mom and Dad will get back together.

Because children long for the family to be together, they will often try to get their parents to be with each other. The children may plot for their parents to meet at their basketball game "by accident." Or they may try to start a fight between their parents, thinking that it is better for the parents to be fighting than not to have any contact at all.

Children who have a normal, healthy bond with their parents will nonetheless feel, at this age, a fear of being abandoned by their parents. This is part of normal development. It shows a strong attachment and the need for parents. Early school-age children will test their parents to be sure the parents are not going to leave them. This "test" can take the form of rejection, such as "I want a divorce from you, Dad!" Hearing this can make a parent mad or sad. If you know that this behavior is a normal part of the child's developmental stage, however, you can more easily step back and say what the child most wants to hear: "Pamela, I will never leave you. I divorced your mother, not you. I love you very much. I will be here for you always." You may have to say this over and over. Because of the divorce, the normal fear of being left is even stronger. Say it until your children believe it. Then say it again.

Do not ever tell your children that you do not want them or that you will leave them. Don't use it as a threat if they misbehave. Don't say it even if you are mad and really do feel like leaving them. This is poison—not just fumes, but poison! It will harm your children. If you feel the urge to say this, resist and keep quiet. Say something else. Think of your children's future.

Children at this age will be able to tell the difference between how their family acts and other families. Most will have a tough time with the changes in their family after divorce. They want the family back the way it was. As with younger children, even a very small bit of hope will make them feel that their parents are getting back together. These children can feel torn between their two parents. It is hard for them to know how to love both parents without taking sides. You may need to give permission. "It's okay to love both of us, Parker. You don't have to take sides. We both love you, too."

School-age children this age may think about the divorce a lot. They may worry that one parent may never return or that one parent doesn't love them anymore. You may even see anger. "You made Dad leave!" As always, telling and showing your children that you love them is very important. You may need to continue offering simple explanations about divorce. Avoid blaming the other parent. And, as always, keep conflict from the children. Don't let them breathe the fumes.

Here are some issues to watch for at this stage:

- Difficulty concentrating at school, home, or church
- Demanding behavior
- Problems sharing—time or things
- Uncooperative
- Taking on adult roles (don't slip into allowing this; your child needs to be a child)

Parents with children in this stage should do the following:
- Listen to and accept children's feelings.
- Give the children time to work on feelings. Don't rush them.
- Use play to work on feelings. It's amazing what a good

conversation you can have about feelings while shooting hoops or drawing or playing checkers.

- Help children express anger safely. For example, "Don't yell at me or your sister if you are mad about the divorce. Go run around the block. Or hit this clown balloon. It's okay to be angry, but anger has to have a safe way out."
- Set a routine schedule, and keep it.

Don't offer hope that you and your coparent will get back together. While it may feel as if you are soothing your children, it is not helpful.

Tips for Parenting School-Age Children

- Set and maintain a consistent schedule and routine is necessary so the child can focus on the job of school, friends, and team activities.

- With your coparent, select activities that match the child's interests, and work together to balance these activities with the demands of school.

- Be flexible. Birthday parties and other peer activities will be important and may require some additional transportation and flexibility of parenting time.

- Provide support for the child's school program by setting a study routine and communicating with the teacher.

- Consider adjusting the time-sharing schedule. Fewer midweek transitions now make it easier for finishing school projects, but both parents need to participate fully. Research shows that children with fathers involved in their schooling perform better in school.

Eleven Years to Thirteen Years: School and Friends

Children at this age are learning to move away from their parents. Many of the things they do (especially those that are annoying to you) are meant to put distance between you. "I am my own person" is the message at this age. Family becomes less important than friends. At age eleven, most children will be very critical of their parents. By age thirteen or fourteen, you may hear or feel that your children are embarrassed to be seen with you. This is very normal. Your children may even be embarrassed by your divorce and not mention it to their friends.

At this age children will resist a new partner in your life. They are becoming aware of sex. The idea of you having sex with someone at all, much less someone who is not their other parent, can be very upsetting to them. You may find your children actively trying to keep you from dating after the divorce. Your children want to keep the family as it is.

Preteens and young teens can sometimes talk to another trusted adult more easily than a parent. You may want to encourage them to talk to such an adult about their feelings. Extended family members, such as aunts or uncles, school counselors, youth group leaders, and athletic coaches can be good sources. If the adult is someone other than a trusted family member, be sure to check the person out first, however. Your child is still young and vulnerable.

Here are some issues to watch for at this stage:

- Anger at parents for the divorce: "You ruined my life"
- Blaming one parent; siding with the "good" parent
- Acting out: lying, skipping school, stealing, or fighting
- Poor grades in school

- Physical problems caused by anxiety: stomachaches or headaches
- Rigid "either/or" thinking
- Trying to be a friend (rather than a child) to one or both parents
- Sexual behavior

Parents with children in this stage should do the following:

- Keep up with regular doctor's appointments. Don't forget to check for orthodontics and skincare needs, since appearances are so important at this age.
- Allow your children to talk about their feelings. Don't criticize or react like you're shocked.
- Keep explaining the divorce.
- Encourage the children to talk to another trusted adult about the divorce.
- Show and tell your children that you love them.
- Remain in your parenting role with your children. They need a parent, not a friend. As much as you may need a friend, resist. Stay a parent. Stay in charge.

Points to Remember When Designing a Plan for a Preteen or Young Teen

- Parenting plans must provide frequent, meaningful contact with both parents.

- Preteen children and young teens do well with many different options of parenting plans as long as the contact is structured and consistent. When possible, plans should include contact during the school week and on weekends so that both parents may be active participants in school and leisure activities.

- Schedules can provide longer times away from either parent (up to a week) but must take into consideration the child's activities and school responsibilities.

- Children should be given open telephone or computer access to the other parent and be given privacy for their calls.

- Rules and routine between the households should have some consistency and continuity for increased success.

- Develop a format for discussing the child's academic and extra-curricular activities without including the child in discussions (journal, email communication, phone conference, "business-like" meeting).

- Children can be consulted about their views and suggestions, but the parents should still make the final decision.

Thirteen to Fifteen Years: Ups and Downs

Children between thirteen and fifteen use the family as a base for support and guidance. Even though your children might not say or show it, they need you as a parent for comfort and structure.

Maturity can vary widely at this age. Girls tend to mature earlier than boys, but both boys and girls will mature at their own pace. As I sometimes tell families, if you have seen one fourteen-year-old, you have seen one fourteen-year-old. Don't assume that your child will be exactly the same teen as your older children when she reaches fourteen.

Your children are turning into young adults. Their bodies are changing, which probably makes them shy around you and other adults. You may see mood swings as hormonal changes occur. What seems like a small problem to you may be seen by your teen as the biggest problem he has ever faced. Emotions can run high (and low) in the space of a few minutes. Stay calm; this, too, will pass. Your young teen needs your stability to manage the physical and emotional overload she is feeling. In addition to experiencing hormonal changes, children at this age seem to be tired in the morning but wired at night. Since school starts early for most children, this can be a problem. Set a "lights out/phones off" time and enforce it. Even if your child is not sleeping, at least he is resting in a dark room.

At this age, children want to have a say in things that matter to them. They may argue with you about everything (it seems so, at least), loudly and at length. Listen, but set limits. For example, "We will talk about this for five minutes, and then we will move on. I may change my mind while we talk, and I may not. I am the parent, however, and I have the majority vote." Your children are learning to control their own lives. Give them some flexibility, but have structure and rules they can fall back on.

This is also the age where peers are more important than parents. Given a choice, your children will likely choose to spend time with their friends rather than with you. This is not personal, or a statement that your children no longer love you. It is the natural moving-away process of learning to live as an independent person. You can set up family times in the schedule, or arrange family outings with friends going along. You may also decide to set a rule that family outing costs, such as movie tickets, are paid by parents, while activities with friends are paid using the children's allowance. Allow your children to stretch their wings while staying involved with the family.

The line that parents walk during this stage is between supporting their child's independence and maintaining a basic structure and close contact with both parents. Remain firm, fair, and loving, and the line will be easier to walk. This stage is not easy for any parent. Complicating this time is the child's exposure to risk: friends who are drinking or smoking, using drugs, or experimenting with sexual behavior. It is vital that you keep the lines of communication open. Don't assume that the school or church is teaching your child what she needs to know about how her body is changing, how to avoid drugs, or what to do about her sexual feelings. Keep talking. Keep listening.

Normal mood swings can turn into angry outbursts and negativity. Children at this age may begin to hide out or stay away from others if they can't figure out how to cope. Sometimes school difficulties begin now as classes become harder, with more demands for homework and extra projects that cut into peer activities. You may see lying, sneakiness, and risky behaviors. Outright defiance can be a concern.

Tips for Parenting Early Teens

- Develop flexible, creative parenting plans. Plans that would not have worked for younger children may work well now.

- While both parents may have less time with the child at home as school and activities increase, increase your contact by being there—at athletic events, performances, academic events, and other activities.

- Work to maintain frequent communication with your teen. Children may try to play one parent against the other. Consider communicating by using a journal, email, phone calls, or "business-like" meetings.

Fifteen to Eighteen Years: Independence with Guidance

Teenagers are preparing to leave home during these years. School, friends, and work will likely come before family. Teens want privacy. They want to make their own decisions. As a parent, you'll need to balance the teen's need for guidance versus his need for independence.

It is important that you remain the parent. The rules will change, of course, as your teen proves he is able to handle more complicated situations. Your younger children may complain that their teenage sister gets to do more than they do. "That's right," you will tell them. "The rules change as you earn the right for them to change."

It is important to remind teens of how *important* family life is. Teens will want to be active with friends, but they'll still need to make time for family. This is a good time to involve your teen in talks about time-sharing, when she would like to spend time with each parent, and family plans.

Teens will need guidance in the areas of emotions and morals. Teens often don't understand their own feelings or behaviors and need help sorting them out. Their moral code, or their sense of what is right and what is wrong, is also still developing. Understand that your guidance will most likely not be asked for or appreciated. Giving it is still your job, however. The satisfying part of parenting is watching your teen grow into a responsible adult. Consider this mother's experience:

When my daughter was twenty, she had a summer job as a nanny/tutor for three very active young boys, all under ten years old. One day she called me out of the blue and said, "Mom, do you remember the time you were telling me to do my summer reading and do my math workbook, and I rolled my eyes, called you mean and stupid, and ran upstairs and slammed my bedroom door? Well, I called to apologize. One of the boys did that to me today, and I could barely stop myself from smacking him in the face. Only the memory of you being so calm with me got me through. Thanks for being a great mom." Now that's the gift of parenting that gives back.

Here are some issues to watch for at this stage:
- Sexual acting-out
- Fighting, name-calling, picking fights
- Fearful of dating
- Feeling embarrassed about changes in the family
- Worried about money and how the family will get along due to the divorce
- Feeling rejected and neglected

Parents at this stage should do the following:
- Show and tell your teens that you love them.
- Set rules, and keep them. Adapt older rules so they are age-appropriate.
- Have adult friends of your own so you don't use your child as a friend.
- Let your teens know it is okay to be different from you.
- Let your teens know it is okay to love both parents after the divorce.

Tips for Parenting Older Teens
- Be aware of the adolescent's need to be consulted, informed, and involved when making the schedule and family plans.

- When setting parenting times and schedules, take into consideration school demands, job hours, automobile access, as well as extracurricular and social activities.
- Remember that adolescents need to balance independent social time with peers and meaningful family time.

The Road Ahead

Each of your children will react differently to a divorce. First-born children act in one way, the baby of the family in another. Some children seem to be born with a smile and follow all the rules. Other children, it seems, are rebels from the cradle. But all children will generally follow the developmental stages listed here. When what you are doing as a parent is not working, check to see if your child might have moved into a new stage. Understanding these stages help keep you on track as a parent.

At Every Age It Is Important to Remember . . .

- Children develop best when both parents have meaningful and stable involvement in their lives.
- Each parent has different and valuable contributions to make to their children's development.
- It is better for young children to spend more time with parents and less time with other caregivers.
- Communication and cooperation between parents is important. Setting consistent rules in both households and sharing knowledge of events create a sense of security for children of all ages. Parents must discuss and plan school activities and other events.

- If children are allowed to bring their personal items back and forth between the households, they develop a better sense of ownership and responsibility. Parents should purchase special things for the children but not restrict those items to their own house.

- Children need to be protected from adult conflicts. They should not be exposed to arguments, hostility, and negative comments between the parents. They do not want to hear negative things about someone they love.

- Children should not be messengers—they are the children. The parents should do the adult work so that children may complete the tasks of being children.

CHAPTER THREE

Nuts and Bolts of Parenting Coordination

This chapter explains the nuts and bolts of parenting coordination: court orders, confidentiality, communication, contracts, fees, and areas to avoid. Why this much detail? Because parenting coordination is something different. The Parenting Coordinator is not a judge, or a lawyer, or a therapist. The Parenting Coordinator doesn't fit in any of the roles you are used to working with in a divorce. This chapter will spell out the details so that you can work better with a Parenting Coordinator.

How Did We Get Here?

A Parenting Coordinator becomes involved with a family when the parents are just not able to get along well enough to parent their children effectively. It's as simple as that. The court may have flagged the parents as "high conflict": angry, hostile, and unable to agree on anything. Or a family therapist may have suggested a Parenting Coordinator after months of work have failed to produce any progress in developing a parenting plan.

Do any of these high-conflict behaviors sound familiar to you?

- Holding back or delaying support payments
- Changing divorce lawyers often
- Taking lots of non-legal issues to court
- Refusing to give the other parent information about the children's health, schooling, or other activities
- Last-minute changes in plans designed to make it hard for the other parent
- Distrust of the other parent
- Bitter anger at the other parent
- Constant arguing about things that can't be proved
- False reports to police and courts about drug use, violence, or criminal activity

When a court, therapist, or lawyer sees these red flags, the result may be a referral to a Parenting Coordinator. Many courts have "early warning" systems set up to help families limit conflict and encourage cooperation. This keeps parents out of the court system except as really needed, and not for nuisance issues. The benefits extend to areas other than legal, as well. The Parenting Coordinator becomes the GPS for the family, helping to set a plan to keep the children on track.

The Court Order and Conflicts

The court order for divorcing parents to use a Parenting Coordinator is sometimes called the "order of referral or appointment." Court orders vary depending on where you live. The court order is a legal document that lists those involved: parents, children, attorneys, and the person who will be the Parenting Coordinator. The court order then sets out the rights of everyone in the process and lists what the Parenting Coordinator is expected to do in working with the family.

The court order is a legal directive. It is not a suggestion. It is not something you can decide not to do after a few weeks. If the court has ordered parenting coordination, your job is to work with the Parenting Coordinator.

Most courts have a list of qualified Parenting Coordinators. The court may assign the Parenting Coordinator or, attorneys for the parents and sometimes the parents themselves may select a Parenting Coordinator from the list. In most cases, the Parenting Coordinator can be changed if *both* parents agree on the change and the court approves it.

The Parenting Coordinator can also be changed if there is a conflict of interest. A conflict of interest happens when the Parenting Coordinator cannot treat both parents the same—the person cannot be objective. Read the example below. Is this a conflict or not?

The Parenting Coordinator first assigned to divorcing parents Bill and Eve was Steve Smith, a qualified Parenting Coordinator and psychologist. Dr. Smith had seen Eve for counseling last year but was no longer her therapist.

Even though therapists are trained to be objective, the *appearance* of possible favoritism could be a conflict of interest. Bill could say, for example, "You take Eve's side because you know her better. You are not listening to what I have to say." Bill might be wrong about the Parenting Coordinator taking sides, but Bill can't help but believe there might be some bias. The Parenting Coordinator should be neutral. Like Switzerland, the Parenting Coordinator does not take sides in the war between the parents.

If you are assigned to a Parenting Coordinator who you think might not be neutral, speak up right away. Don't wait.

Talk to the Parenting Coordinator about it. Most conflicts are due to a Parenting Coordinator having two roles with one of the parents. Here are some likely conflicts:

- The Parenting Coordinator is also your attorney, custody evaluator, therapist, or mediator.
- The Parenting Coordinator was your supervisor at work a few years ago.
- Your ex owns a lawn maintenance company that takes care of the Parenting Coordinator's lawn at the office and at home.
- The Parenting Coordinator coaches your child's soccer team.

It might not be possible to avoid a conflict if you live in an area with limited professional services. People who live in rural areas may have little choice, since the only psychologist in town could also be the Parenting Coordinator—and someone who reads to preschoolers at the library, runs a children's choir, and volunteers at the domestic violence safe house. Conflict just can't be avoided in such cases. However, a good Parenting Coordinator will talk about the situation right away. She will set boundaries that will help keep her work with you as neutral as possible.

Another possible area of conflict is bartering. Parenting Coordinators usually charge fees that are paid by both parents. Bartering is trading Parenting Coordinator services for something else. For example, I was court ordered to be the Parenting Coordinator for a family who had not done well with their first Parenting Coordinator. In this case, the father owned a nice restaurant. The father had traded meals at his restaurant for parenting coordination services with the previous Parenting

Coordinator. The mother, when she found out about this, complained to the court right away. She thought the Parenting Coordinator was biased toward the father because of the trading arrangement. You can see that even the appearance of bias can be a problem.

Being neutral means that you should not try to tip the balance to your side by bringing gifts or trying to do favors for the Parenting Coordinator. The Parenting Coordinator will not take any gifts you bring him. He will also refuse favors. Gifts or favors can be seen as trying to get the Parenting Coordinator on your side. Even the appearance of bias is not good. Save the gifts for your child's teacher or dance instructor.

Confidentiality

Parenting coordination is usually not confidential, but this varies based on where you live. That might seem like an odd thing to say. We are used to therapists, ministers, and lawyers who are restricted from telling others what is said to them in appointments. But parenting coordination is different. For one thing, it may be court ordered. This means that the court may request reports about progress or the lack of progress in the appointments. Some courts require the Parenting Coordinator to report if the parents are not able to reach agreement about important parenting decisions or will not attend appointments that the Parenting Coordinator sets up.

Some courts may ask for regular written reports from the Parenting Coordinator. These reports may list conflicts, solutions, and changes to the parenting plan. In this way, the court is kept up-to-date on whether parents are following the parenting schedule and Parenting Plan. Copies of the reports are usually sent to both parents and their attorneys. Everyone involved sees the reports. There are no secret reports that only the judge or one attorney gets. This open plan means that one parent cannot reasonably conclude that others are doing things behind his back. It keeps everything out in the open—but only for those involved in the situation: courts, attorneys, and parents.

Sometimes the Parenting Coordinator is asked to appear in court. The Parenting Coordinator will usually only agree to this in order to provide progress updates or if the judge insists. The Parenting Coordinator does not want to be an expert witness. This would run the risk of the Parenting Coordinator looking as if she were biased toward one of the parents. Most Parenting Coordinators will give "facts only" to the court.

For example, if I am called to court and one of the attorneys asks me if the father is attending sessions and offering helpful suggestions to resolve parenting disputes. I will not give details. I will only give facts. "The father has missed two appointments and attended eight appointments" might be what I tell the judge.

The other area where questions of confidentiality arise concerns the reports to and from team members. In parenting coordination, the parents are not the only stakeholders. Teachers, therapists, dentists, doctors, and others are also involved. They all need information to do their jobs. Likewise, the Parenting Coordinator needs information from other team members to know what they have done and what still needs to be done. These reports are usually treated confidentially, meaning the Parenting Coordinator may not share everything with all team members or with the parents. Listed below are some of the people who might be on the team:

- Attorney
- Teacher, tutor
- Therapist
- Parenting class instructor
- Anger management group leader
- Doctor
- Dentist, orthodontist
- Child care worker, nanny
- Coach
- Extended family

Let's talk about that last one—extended family. You would not expect a written report from Pamela's grandmother on how the trip to the zoo went. But her grandmother may be a member of the team. I often tell grandparents, "Don't stand outside the circle. Come in and help." Family can be a big help in a divorce. They can offer a sense of safety to children with familiar faces and routines. The children know that some parts of their lives will not change. Grandma is still picking them up on Thursdays for pizza night, as always.

Because Grandma is a part of the team, the Parenting Coordinator may need to speak with her about a problem that Pamela is having. Or it may be necessary to ask Grandma to please stick to the schedule set out in the parenting plan. The Parenting Coordinator will not tell family members more than is needed, however. Confidentiality will be kept as much as possible. Family members will only be told what they need to know about caring for the children.

Confidentiality goes both ways. You also must be careful not to talk about what goes on in parenting coordination appointments except in a general way. "We are working out the parenting plan" is all you should say. Then change the subject. It is too easy to slip and give out details that can hurt the planning process. So, while you might be tempted to give the juicy details to your girlfriend or fishing buddy . . . don't.

Most of all, do not tell your children details of parenting coordination appointments. They do not need to know that your ex-wife screamed at you and called you an "ass****" during the session. Yes, it's a great story. And it would make you feel good for a few minutes to tell it. But remember the fumes. Your children don't need to breathe the fumes of their mother's anger or your satisfaction that she lost control.

Many Parenting Coordinators take notes during sessions and may give both you and your coparent a copy, either as the appointment concludes or later via email or regular mail. The notes will contain agreements you have both made during the session. Changes in the parenting plan will be noted. Speak up right away if you see something in the notes that doesn't correspond with your memory of what happened. Be aware that you may not remember everything accurately if you were in a highly emotional state.

Keep the session notes somewhere that others cannot find them easily and read them. This means not leaving the notes on the seat in your car, on top of your dresser, or on the kitchen counter. Take a minute to put them someplace out of the way.

It's also important to be somewhat discreet about the work you are doing during parenting coordination sessions. Consider the experience of this Parenting Coordinator:

A father I was working with in parenting coordination sessions saw me at a fund-raiser we were both attending. The fund-raiser was in a large ballroom at a local hotel.

He came up to me in a group of people and started asking questions about a court hearing that was coming up.

Public settings are not the place to talk about parenting coordination. Too many people can overhear. In fact, your Parenting Coordinator may act as if he does not know you when in public. This is on purpose. He is respecting your privacy. Keep your boundaries and don't try to talk to him in public.

Confidentiality does not apply during parenting coordination sessions, however. Information from one parent may be shared with the other parent if the Parenting Coordinator meets with each parent separately. This gives the Parenting Coordinator the chance to hear both sides and get more information, if needed. Any reports from other team members that is shared with one parent will also be shared with the other parent. For example, the counselor hired by the mother may report on Parker's progress. The report will be shared with both the mother and father.

To sum up: confidentiality in parenting coordination applies *outside* the team of parents, Parenting Coordinator, the court, attorneys, and professional team members. Among this group, information will be shared. Outside this group—which includes your children—confidentiality will be maintained.

The Power of the Parenting Coordinator

As I said earlier, the court order is just that—an order, not a suggestion. This means that the court has given the Parenting Coordinator power to make decisions with you—and for you, if you and your coparent cannot agree. The Parenting Coordinator will explain her role at the beginning of your work with her. She has responsibilities to your children (first), the court (second), and then to you and your coparent. Remember that the children are the focus of parenting coordination. The court often gives the Parenting Coordinator "decision-making (called arbitration in some areas) authority" to solve really difficult problems. Sometimes the parents themselves give the Parenting Coordinator decision-making power because it is easier on everyone.

As I have said before, this is handled differently depending on where you live. However, most jurisdictions give the Parenting Coordinator these powers:

- Creating a parenting plan with both parents (if one isn't already in place)
- Being sure that children can be with both parents
- Protecting the rights of the children
- Making sure the parenting plan is followed
- Changing the parenting plan (add details to agreements to assist with implementation or adding agreements as new parenting issues arise)
- Creating ways to coparent that will reduce conflict
- Referring parents to needed services: therapy, parenting courses, anger management groups, and so on
- Referring children to needed services: therapy, tutors, doctors, dentists, and so on

With these powers the Parenting Coordinator stays neutral. Remember that the primary focus is the children. The Parenting Coordinator is not, however, a custody evaluator. In order to remain neutral, the Parenting Coordinator would not advise the court on which parent is best for the children's primary residence. In this case being neutral is also the best for the children. Studies repeatedly show that children do best being with both parents on some type of regular schedule.

There is one situation that is an exception to being neutral and confidential: abuse. If a parent abuses or is violent toward a child or the other parent, the Parenting Coordinator is legally required to report it right away. This is true across the United States (though Canada does not currently have this same reporting law). The Parenting Coordinator has the power in most areas to modify the parenting plan for the safety of the children; the Parenting Coordinator would inform the court of this change right away. Supervised visits may be required. In a supervised visit, the parent sees the children with another adult present.

The Contract

Both you and your coparent will likely sign a contract with the Parenting Coordinator. Why sign a contract when there is a court order? The court order sets the basics for parenting coordination, but not the details. The court order specifies what authority the Parenting Coordinator has, what the court expects will happen, and what kind of information the Parenting Coordinator will be able to get from doctors, therapists, and others on the team. The parenting coordination contract, on the other hand, is a professional services agreement. It defines the role and responsibilities of the Parenting Coordinator (and the parents) in detail. Think of the court order as the frame of a house and the parenting coordination contract as the walls and roof.

Most contracts are written in non-legal language so they are easy to understand. Some even include a glossary of legal terms that might be used in court so the parents will understand what the attorneys and judge are saying. The contract will set the term of the agreement—how long it will last—and state how the contract can be ended. Two years is an average term for this type of contract.

The role of the Parenting Coordinator is spelled out in detail in the contract. This is necessary because Parenting Coordinators may act outside their traditional professional roles. The Parenting Coordinator may be a lawyer, but will not give legal advice. The Parenting Coordinator may be a therapist, but will not provide counseling. Or the Parenting Coordinator may be a mediator, but will not provide mediation services. It is important from the very beginning to set out the role of the Parenting Coordinator.

The contract will lay out how and when appointments will be made and what will happen for no-show appointments. Procedures for rescheduling and canceling appointments will be defined, with consequences that apply to both parents.

The contract will also encompass confidentiality limits, how needed information will be obtained, how to communicate with the Parenting Coordinator between appointments, how the Parenting Coordinator will report to parents, and other details on how parenting coordination works. Covering these fine points in the contract helps avoid surprises as well as game playing by one or both parents.

Fees

Parents pay for parenting coordination fees. Usually both parents pay. Parenting coordination laws usually require the court to make sure the parents can afford the fees. The contract will set out the fees, how to pay, and what happens if payments are late. Most Parenting Coordinators charge an hourly rate. The rate includes not only time in sessions with parents, but also time spent with team members. Appointments may be face-to-face or occur virtually, by using a webcam or conference meeting service. Telephone calls, reading emails, responding to emails, creating reports, preparing for court visits, and copying records are all billed.

Some Parenting Coordinators ask for a retainer. This is a sum of money paid up front that is drawn down as time is charged. Others work on a pay-as-you-go system. Either way, the billing should be clearly stated in the contract. Ask if you have any questions.

Let me talk for a moment about fees. The fees you pay for parenting coordination are an investment in your children. If you and your coparent could work out a parenting plan by yourselves, you would have already done that. The reality is that you need professional help. Whether it is your coparent who cannot agree, yourself, or both of you, the professional Parenting Coordinator is the expert you need—for the sake of your children. Your children are the focus. They are why you need a Parenting Coordinator.

Common Mistakes

GPS systems don't work if you don't pay attention to them. But this is not an easy time for you to pay attention. Emotions are high, finances are tight, and everywhere you turn someone else wants your attention—now.

Take a deep breath. Your children need you to pay attention right now. Yes, contracts and parenting plans require focusing on lots of detail. Yes, there are a lot of things to learn and things to do. Make parenting coordination a priority. Be sure you understand the contract. Ask your attorney to look it over, if you like. Make time for appointments, and be there. I don't mean just be there physically. Be there to pay attention to what is going on and to how this process can help your children.

So, the first common mistake is not taking the process seriously. It is an investment of your time, money, and attention. Make it a good investment. It will go better—and more quickly, by the way—if you are really part of the process.

The second common mistake is not understanding the Parenting Coordinator's role. Paying attention in the first sessions will help with this. But it is easy to slip into thinking of the Parenting Coordinator as a therapist or an attorney. This is not marriage therapy. Don't bring up your feelings about things your coparent has done in the past. This is also not a legal session. Don't think of sessions as a place to get everything you can from your coparent.

"I need to air my feelings about my ex" —*not here.*

"I should get a fair deal" —*children get the fair deal, not you or your ex.*

Parenting coordination really is different from what you have experienced up until now. Be prepared to learn a new way to relate to a professional in the divorce process. I tell parents that this is a safe a place where they can work out a plan for their children.

In thinking of parenting coordination as therapy, parents often don't want to meet together. Yet, unless there is violence in the relationship, meeting together is the best way to work out the parenting plan. Just trust me on this. As painful as a joint meeting may be, it works. Setting up and putting a plan in place is not easy. But it works. Things will get better. Your children will benefit from your hard work now.

Because the Parenting Coordinator is not acting in a medical role, she will usually not take "emergency" calls about your coparent's behavior. Parents should plan ahead and then follow the plan. The Parenting Coordinator will give you information about what to do if your coparent becomes violent. Don't hesitate to call a domestic violence hotline or 911. (See chapter 7 for more on dealing with violent behavior.) Violence, as I have said before, should never wait to be reported.

Another common mistake is not speaking up right away if the Parenting Coordinator has a conflict of interest in taking your case. We talked earlier about the Parenting Coordinator who has provided professional services to you or your coparent in the past (or even now), works for one of you, or is bartering for services. But a conflict can also be one of ideas. Take, for example, a Parenting Coordinator who tries to influence your religious beliefs. This should never happen. The Parenting Coordinator should be neutral in all areas. Consider what happened in this case:

A couple in Sarasota was divorcing because the father had come out as a gay man. The Parenting Coordinator said in a session, "Homosexuals should never be parents," laughed, and said she was only joking. The father asked the court to change the Parenting Coordinator due to her bias. The court agreed immediately. The court gave the Parenting Coordinator a warning to maintain neutrality when working with other parents.

Parenting coordination is new territory for most people reading this book. But if you invest in the process, you will find that it can be a valuable resource for you and your children.

CHAPTER FOUR

Setting the Route

Parenting Coordinator Steps

Parenting coordination is more time and cost effective when the Parenting Coordinator follows specific steps to set up the parenting plan. Your input, as a parent, is the key to keeping the process moving. Most Parenting Coordinators will begin sessions with a contract review and an overview of the process. Next up is to gather information about you and your family. The Parenting Coordinator will spend some time asking about you and your ex as parents, your children, the unique needs of your family, sources of conflict, and resources available. The Parenting Coordinator is looking for how you and your coparent act with each other and your ways of handling conflict, in order to develop the best plan for you.

Fastest Route, Shortest Route

The other important task is one that may crop up several times. This is distinguishing "real" issues from surface issues. You know how this works. Your coparent says that you don't answer the phone when she tries to call the kids when they are with you. You go out of your way to make sure your cell phone battery is charged, that it is in your pocket and not in silent mode, and the kids are available at the agreed-upon time for calling, but it doesn't seem to help. Why won't your coparent stop bugging you about telephone contact with the kids?

The issue may not be the phone check-ins. Phone check-in is just the "surface" issue. The real issue, the one your coparent doesn't want to admit to or may not have admitted to herself, is that she still has hope that you might come back into the marriage one day. She may want the contact to be sure that you aren't seeing another woman. Identifying the "real" or below the surface issues allows the Parenting Coordinator to set the shortest route for the journey, just as a GPS would. In this scenario, the Parenting Coordinator might meet with your ex alone and suggest that she seek counseling to help her deal with unresolved feelings about the breakup of the marriage. Making detours around surface issues will only slow down the process. On the other hand, if you and your coparent have agreed on a time for her to talk to the children on the phone each day when they are with you and you consistently "forget," then the real issue is what motivates you to violate the agreement that you know will provoke a response from her.

Remember that the Parenting Coordinator is not a therapist. Looking for real issues is done to call attention to them so the work of the parenting plan can move ahead. The Parenting Coordinator might also point out a style of communication that is getting in the way. Consider this example:

> *The Parenting Coordinator says to the parents, "When you speak to or about each other, I hear contempt—an utter disrespect for this relationship. But we have work to do. Think of this as a business relationship. Your business is your children. Let's agree to follow what we agreed on when we started—what is in the best interests of your children."*

You might be thinking, "That's easy for you to say. I really do feel contempt for my ex. What should I do, fake it?" My answer to you is "yes." I often tell parents to "fake it 'til you make it" if that's the best you can do in the beginning. This means acting in a way that's different from how you feel. Your attitude will follow your behavior. Or not. If it never does—if you still feel contempt for your ex—then just keep faking it. Actors do this all the time. Your Best Actor award will be the health of your children. You will also enable the parenting coordination process to move more quickly and smoothly if you avoid throwing verbal grenades into the conversations and purposefully derailing the process.

Please understand that I am *not* asking you to change your feelings. You have those feelings. But you don't have to act on them. You don't have to show them at all except when you choose to. Hopefully, that will be with a counselor or other trusted advisor. You are in control of how and when you communicate your feelings.

The communication skills you learn in parenting coordination sessions can, and *should*, be used in talking to your children about your ex. You can learn to manage how and when you communicate your feelings. Remember the fumes. Use your neutral face and neutral language when talking with your children. Children learn by listening and watching. It is best they learn that their parents are not about angry looks, contempt, and name-calling. Give your children a chance for normal dating and marriage by modeling healthy, respectful communication.

Parenting Coordinator may point out not only what you say, but also how your body language is communicating what you feel. We all communicate more with our bodies than with words.

Scientists estimate that most communication is nonverbal. This means that you need to pay attention to both what you say and how you say it. Otherwise, you may be oozing contempt (or anger, or hate).

Many people are unaware of what their body language is saying. The key to managing body language is to *pay attention* to it. Notice how you are sitting or standing, where your arms are, and what your facial muscles are doing. Here are some tips on negative body language so that you can begin to recognize and avoid it:

- Look at your ex when either of you is speaking. Make yourself look your ex in the eye when greeting, talking, and, especially, when listening.

- But . . . don't stare. Blink normally. Nod your head to show agreement. Pay attention to be sure you are not unconsciously shaking your head "no." This happens more often than you might think—watch for it.

- Don't fidget. It gives the message that you are bored and not paying attention. This includes drumming your fingers, scratching, darting your eyes around the room, squirming in your chair . . . you get the idea. Sit still.

- Stand and sit up straight. A slumped posture signals defeat.

- Don't hide your hands, especially your palms. People with secrets don't show their hands. The most open way to keep your hands visible is to set them in your lap with the palms up.

- But . . . be careful that your hands are not in fists. This conveys an obvious "I am angry enough to punch" message.

- Don't fold your arms across your chest. This posture says "I have made up my mind and you can't change it." Crossing your legs at the knee or ankle is fine, however.

- Pay attention to your expression. Do you feel the furrow between your eyebrows when you listen to, or talk about, your ex? Do you notice your mouth turning down in an automatic frown? If the best you can do is a neutral expression—not mad and not happy—then put on your neutral face. You may need to watch yourself in a mirror. You might be surprised at what expressions your face takes on when you think about your ex. Practice the neutral expression, a business-like expression, or an interested look until you can put on that expression whenever needed.

The Parenting Coordinator will call out behaviors that get in the way of working on the parenting plan. One of these is blame. Playing the "blame game" is not helpful—not at all. If you are focused on proving that your ex is to blame, stop right now. Widen your viewpoint so you can look at your children. Blaming your ex hurts your children. They will learn from you that relationships are one-sided. They will learn that they don't need to examine their own behavior, because they will be looking at the other person's behavior and blaming him. This is a pattern scientists have seen again and again in studies on the effects of divorce. Children learn what they see from you.

My recommendation to you is that you delete the word "fault" from your vocabulary. Put a sign up on your refrigerator:

> *Learn to*
> *let things*
> *you can't*
> *control...*
>
> *...go*

Then move on with your parenting plan. If you find yourself focusing on your ex and trying to get others to blame her with you, let the alarm bells ring in your mind. Or if you find yourself saying "always" or "never" about your ex, stop to consider the facts. Consider this mother's complaint:

> *Bill never spent any time with the kids. He was more interested in his career and hanging out with his friends than in being a dad.*

The fact may be that Bill had to work two jobs to support the family. Yes, he worked a lot. But it is not true that he *never* spent time with your children. When you hear yourself say "always" or "never," pay attention. These are words that also could be deleted from your vocabulary. It is too easy to use these words to place blame on your ex.

Think about it this way. Your children know that they are part of both of you. They may think, "If I am made of Mom and Dad, then when Mom says Dad is awful, I must be awful too." Walk away from the blame game. No one wins.

Avoid Toll Roads

The reason for all this attention on communication is because parenting coordination sessions require a lot of communication between you and your ex, as well as you and the Parenting Coordinator. Much of what you will be talking about will be conflict areas. It is much easier, and cheaper, to solve these conflicts in parenting coordination sessions than in court. Court is the "toll road" in this process—the cost is high, and the exits are few.

Common sources of conflict among divorcing or newly divorced parents are family, money, religion, discipline, education, and dating or remarriage. All of these areas can carry emotional baggage from parenting issues that were never solved while you were married. Now you and your coparent have to deal with them in order to work out the parenting plan.

The larger family—grandparents, aunts and uncles, and cousins—can be a large source of conflict. How will they be worked into the parenting plan? Will they be helpful or hurtful? Some family members take sides, and can breathe fumes on your children just as you or your ex might. The Parenting Coordinator may ask family members to attend a session or two so they can understand their part in the parenting plan.

Money can be a source of conflict in obvious and not-so-obvious ways. If one parent has a more flexible budget, she might buy the children expensive gifts or pay for trips to movies and amusement parks. You, on the other hand, might be struggling to get all the bills paid. Money for dance lessons, judo class, or private school can be a problem also, especially if both parents don't agree that the cost is a worthwhile one.

Religion usually becomes an issue when parents disagree

how the children will be brought up. The level of conflict grows with the level of involvement in the faith and the difference between the two parents' beliefs. A Lutheran and a Methodist will probably find little to argue about. But if Mom is a practicing Catholic and Dad is a devout Muslim, the question of faith for the children becomes more important.

Discipline is an issue because most parents believe that their children are a reflection of how good a parent they have been. An acting-out child must have a "bad" parent, and a child who is well behaved must have a "good" parent. Every parent wants to believe that she is a good parent—certainly a better parent than the ex. Even minor issues become a problem. This is because parenting is labeled as good or bad, instead of an approach or style. Here is an example:

Dave gives the kids macaroni and cheese for dinner every visit. He's a bad parent because that's all he cooks. The kids need different kinds of food, not the same thing every time. He only has to cook one meal during the school week. He could at least fix something healthy.

As you can see, Dave's cooking is labeled as proof of his "bad" parenting, instead of as a different style of parenting. Here is how Dave views the issue:

What Eve doesn't know is that the kids love my mac and cheese. To them, it's a meal that says "Dad cares enough to cook this special meal for us." I serve vegetable juice on ice and give the kids celery sticks as stirrers. It's a fun meal for us. I'm not a gourmet cook, but I do know how to make mac and cheese. It beats taking the kids out for burgers and fries.

Dating and remarriage can put you off course if not handled well. Even though you may think you have no feelings left for your ex, dating or remarriage can bring up all kinds of feelings: regret, jealousy, or anger. The Parenting Coordinator may recommend counseling for you or your coparent if it looks as if there are problems handling what is going on and it affects your parenting.

The next chapter will provide more information on conflict: analysis, identification, and management.

U-Turns

When there is so much going on in your life, it is easy to get distracted and fall back into old habits and behaviors. You may have been angry with your ex for so long that, even after learning how to communicate without getting angry, something will push your button and the anger comes roaring back. Before you know it, you are emitting toxic fumes of anger and contempt.

When you go off course in your car, the GPS helps you get back on track. Often the first thing you hear is "Recalculating," and then "Make a U-turn in 500 feet." With parenting after divorce, the Parenting Coordinator will serve as your GPS and help you when you get off track.

Sometimes the U-turn may not seem necessary. Consider this case:

Every Saturday, Jane's ex-husband, Peter, came over and mowed her lawn. They had agreed to "barter" this service as a way of reducing child support. She always prepared him his favorite meal for dinner. Peter would eat dinner with Jane and their young son. They would talk about what was happening in their lives, tell jokes, and generally have a nice time. Then Peter would leave and go home to his new wife.

What is wrong with this picture? It seems like a good divorce, doesn't it? The problem is, their young son has not been able to adjust to the divorce. Every Saturday, his heart tells him that Mom and Dad are going to get back together. After all, aren't they all sharing a nice dinner? But then Dad leaves, and his hopes are dashed. Next Saturday he gets his hopes up again, only to be disappointed.

Scientific studies have shown that this cycle of hope and despair is very damaging, particularly to young children who aren't able to understand all the reasons behind their parents' behavior. The now-and-then reinforcement of hope that parents will get back together can cause behavioral or emotional problems in children. The child never gets to move on. The parents may be so wrapped up in themselves that they can't see how their behavior affects their child. Often the two ex-spouses are paying more attention to each other than to their child, leaving the child emotionally neglected.

In Las Vegas, people sit at slot machines for hours at a time, pulling the lever again and again. They hold cups of nickels or dimes that they feed into the slot machine. They don't seem to be making a lot of money. Why do you think they do this? It's because slot machines are rewarding the behavior. The reward happens because, every now and then, there is a big payoff. Bells ring, lights flash, and coins come pouring out of the slot.

Scientists call this "intermittent reinforcement." It is the most powerful reward for behavior, and the hardest to break. In a sense, it is addicting. Its power comes from happening every now and then, not every time. So the person keeps doing what causes the reward, even if the reward takes a long time in coming.

The other thing that happens with slot-machine rewards is superstitious behavior and false beliefs. Athletes wear "lucky" socks because they won a big game when wearing those socks. Gamblers blow on the dice because they won big once after doing that. Children are the same. They can develop false beliefs: "If I help Dad mow the lawn, he and Mom will get back together."

Having a good divorce is not the problem. Parents who are merely friendly with one another won't cause this wishful thinking in children. It's parents who are still emotionally locked into each other who can give children the hope that their parents will get back together.

Divorced parents need to have boundaries— separation between each other emotionally. A family with divorced parents who are still locked into one another looks like this:

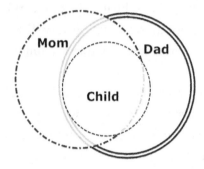

A family with good boundaries allows for closeness, but each person is more himself or herself. That kind of family looks more like this:

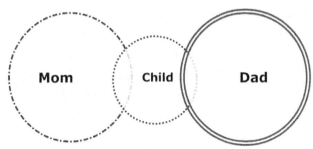

This can be a U-turn point. If you and your ex are too close to each other emotionally, it's time to let go. In a typical divorce, the husband and wife separate from one other, date other people, and perhaps remarry. You may be too close to the problem to see it. The Parenting Coordinator will identify the behavior, point out the impact on your children, and ask you to change the behavior.

The other obvious U-turn is the "still-angry" parent. I have talked a lot about this because it is such a big problem and so many parents are locked in anger. You would think that everyone who is angry would be aware of it. But very often the anger is deep-seated and comes out in odd ways. The angry parent throws up roadblocks to any kind of progress on the parenting plan. As a Parenting Coordinator, I call out this behavior: "In this area, you are not in touch with reality. This is unreasonable behavior." The parent is so angry that he simply is not thinking straight.

The different ways that anger is shown include contempt, criticism, defensiveness, and stonewalling. John Gottman, a psychologist who has studied the communication of couples, calls these the "four horsemen of the apocalypse." In the Bible, the four horsemen were signs that something terrible was just about to happen. Gottman has since added a fifth horseman, belligerence. In parenting coordination, these five communication styles lead to a bad outcome.

Criticism, one of the "horsemen," is not complaining. A complaint is about an action. A criticism is about your ex's character—who he is, not what he has done. Criticisms often use words and phrases that include "never," "always," "you are . . ." and "why do you . . . ?" Read these two examples. Which one is criticism?

A. "Why do you always forget to pick Parker up? My mother had to get him last Tuesday."

B. "You were late picking Parker up from soccer Tuesday. He had to call my mother to get him."

If you picked A, the first example, you're right. A complaint is just facts—"here is what happened . . ." A criticism throws in blame and tries to put down the person's character. You can identify criticism by its "you are" rather than "you did" statements.

Anger is usually about being hurt, disappointed, or betrayed. There is no denying that you were deeply wounded. Your heart was broken and you are emotionally "bleeding" all over the place. But your anger is getting in the way of mending that heart. This is the time to focus on the children. Often counseling is recommended if the anger is just too hard to get past.

Contempt deserves more discussion, though you are well aware by this time how toxic contempt is. Contempt means that you feel disgust for your ex. You can see nothing good in her. Contempt is shown in sarcasm, mockery, name-calling, and hostile jokes. You may think that, because your child laughs when you tell a hostile joke about your ex, it does not hurt your child. You might even think that your child enjoys the joke. But she is only laughing because you expect her to. Children say and do what they think you want to hear and see, because they want your approval and love.

Some parents think that withdrawing or ignoring—what Gottman calls "stonewalling"—is being neutral. It is not. Stonewalling is anger expressed in silence or quietly: not answering, saying a one or two word answer, changing the subject, or leaving the room. The stonewaller distances himself by looking away or down when you are talking. He is trying not to be in the same room with you.

I tell angry parents that holding on to anger toward each other is like drinking poison—and waiting for the other person to die. It doesn't have the effect you want. Forgiveness is a gift you give yourself that also helps your children. Remember, even if you don't feel forgiveness, you can act as if you do.

> "If you want to forget something or someone, never hate it or never hate him/her. Everything and everyone that you hate is engraved upon your heart; if you want to let go of something, if you want to forget, you cannot hate."
> [C. Joybell C.]

One of the four horsemen, defensiveness, is not in the "anger" family but can be just as destructive. Defensiveness is seeing yourself as a victim. Sometimes this is based in reality. Your ex may be critical and attacking. Defending yourself seems like the right thing to do. The problem is that it does not work. It doesn't work because your defense is saying, "The problem is you, not me." This almost always causes your ex to just get angrier.

You can hear defensiveness in making excuses such as "I had to do . . ." or "I wouldn't have done ___ if you had done ____." Cross-complaining is also defensiveness. This is when you return a criticism with one of your own about your ex: "But you do . . ." You can also hear defensiveness in "yes, but" statements, which is a way to sound as if you are going to agree (yes), but then disagreeing (but). Defensiveness can even move into whining—"It's not fair that . . ."—or repeating yourself without listening to your ex.

Studies show that your body undergoes physical changes when you are angry. Your blood pressure goes up. Adrenaline kicks in, which causes the fight-or-flight response. You may sweat or feel your heart rate increase. Your breathing may quicken. In short, your body is in overdrive just when you need it to be in neutral. If you are not aware of this response, you may naturally try to fight by being critical, defensive, or contemptuous. Or you might try flight by stonewalling.

Awareness and prevention are the keys here. Being aware of what might happen can help you to mentally prepare. Sometimes in parenting coordination sessions, I even wear a referee's whistle and blow it when one of the parents communicates poorly. A laugh can sometimes defuse the situation. Once I started singing the first part of the song "Stop in the Name of Love." The parents stared at me for a moment, then burst out laughing. The angry moment passed, and we could start again.

Some people, however, have a very hard time with the physical response to negative communication. Men especially are hardwired for a higher heart rate for longer than women. Studies have shown that a man's heart rate can stay elevated for twenty minutes after an argument. It is difficult to think calmly when your heart is racing. The body is trying hard to keep you angry. Some of my clients have experienced positive results from using deep breathing techniques, similar to what is taught in yoga or meditation. Sometimes we have to fight the body's natural responses in order to break the cycle of anger.

Rules of the Road

Driving is safer and quicker when everyone follows the rules of the road. This is also true in parenting coordination sessions.

Here are some basic rules of the road to follow during these sessions:

- Take turns. When driving, you yield to other cars so that traffic can move smoothly. The same is true when working with your coparent on issues related to your children. Take turns talking. Take turns picking Pamela up after dance class. Take turns compromising. You get the idea.

- Don't tow. Only bring yourself to sessions unless the Parenting Coordinator asks you to bring someone else. You don't need roadies for support.

- Use your signals. Communicate what you are doing, when you are doing it, and how you will be doing it. Be clear. Then be sure to follow up. Don't signal and then not change lanes.

- Only call 911 in an emergency. Don't make small issues into big ones. Don't make false claims that your ex is using drugs or being violent. If you are angry enough to make a false claim, you probably need to see a therapist.

- Arrive on time. Some Parenting Coordinators fine a parent who arrives late. After all, who would stop speeding if there were no fines involved?

- Don't cut off others. In other words, don't interrupt. If you have to, make a note of what you want to say. But don't pay so much attention to your note that you are not listening.

- Share the road. Parenting coordination sessions are almost always held with both parents. This is to make sure that you are both heard and understood. It also prevents either of you from thinking that there is something going on "behind your back." Most Parenting Coordinators will not even take a phone call from one parent between sessions, but will wait until the next session to discuss the issue. Emails from one parent are usually copied to the other parent, as well as replies. This is a shared process.

- Don't speed. Parenting coordination is a process that takes time. Put some time into it. Read the material the Parenting Coordinator gives you as a resource. Prepare for sessions.

Roadblocks

Some couples are so locked into anger that they reach a roadblock and can't go any further. These couples have such a negative view of one another that they avoid any contact. They refuse to communicate directly. Often these couples will say, "We can't stand to be in the same room together." They use others as messengers—attorneys, their children, teachers, and other family members.

These ex-spouses see each other as the "bad guy" in the relationship. They don't want their children to have contact with the other parent. They have such toxic communication that every sentence is peppered with contempt. Here are some examples:

Tell that jerk he can't see the kids this week. He doesn't deserve to see them.

She's crazy. I'm sure she is hurting the kids.

The idiot's new wife is bringing the kids on Saturday.

You may be thinking that this describes a couple in the

first few months after divorce. Unfortunately, some coparents behave this way even years post-divorce. They may have tried counseling and mediation without success. The Parenting Coordinator may have to set up hands-off communication for these parents. Online calendars and communication programs are a no-contact way to handle the children's schedule. Both Mom and Dad can put appointments on the calendar but do not need to speak with each other. The program can be set up so the Parenting Coordinator and attorneys can also view the calendar and see how parents are communicating with one another.

These road blocked parents can also use a journal to communicate information with each other. The journal is for facts only—not feelings. The child might carry the journal but does not write in it. Parents use the journal, either paper or electronic, to be sure important information is shared. "Parker had a fever of 101 last night. He took two Tylenol at 9 p.m. Temperature normal this morning."

Another communication strategy is to use email. Just using email itself is usually not enough to solve the communication problems of road blocked parents, however. I generally begin with having both parents send me an email that is written to their ex. I review the email, edit it for hostile or provocative content, and send it back with "edits" or suggestions on rewording. Why? This helps parents learn how to communicate *neutrally*. Sometimes the communication has been negative for so long that the parents have to relearn how to communicate without name-calling and blaming.

Once the parents have relearned the basics of neutral email, they will send each other emails and also send me a copy so I can monitor their exchanges. This is to help avoid any relapses into angry communication. Eventually the parents learn to communicate facts, not feelings. They learn to solve problems, not create them.

I have worked with couples that started off road blocked and eventually learned to communicate with each other for the sake of their children. It can be a long and expensive process. Learning to talk with one another in healthy ways is much more efficient on so many levels—time, emotional energy, and money.

Some roadblocks, however, are dangerous and require professional help. These include violence, substance abuse, and mental illness. Violence against you or your children should never be tolerated. Even if the violence has ended, you and your children may still be scared and anxious around your ex. The Parenting Coordinator may suggest separate, or "disengaged" parenting, using online calendars and a journal to communicate about the children to be sure that you and your children remain safe and secure.

Substance abuse can be a tricky issue. Some angry parents accuse the other of substance abuse to get even. The ex may have had a problem in the past with drugs or alcohol, but be clean now. Or the ex may have started drinking or using drugs during the divorce process. The Parenting Coordinator will check court records for DUI charges, rehab, or detox. The Parenting Coordinator may refer a parent to a therapist who treats substance abuse.

When one of the parents abuses drugs or alcohol, safety steps must be put in place. The court may order the abuser to have a urine screen before each contact with the children.

Supervised visits may even be ordered. These steps are for the safety of your children.

Having a mental illness does not mean a person cannot be a good parent. It depends on how well controlled the illness is. Just like diabetes, mental illness can often be controlled with medication and behavior change. A diabetic learns to check her insulin levels regularly, eat certain foods and avoid other foods, and take her medication on schedule. In the same way, a person with a mental illness may control the symptoms by taking medication regularly and following certain behavior plans.

Mental illness that affects parenting is the roadblock in many cases of divorce. Care of the children is the main issue. The Parenting Coordinator may ask for mental health treatment records to see how the parent has done in the past. However, the stress of separation and divorce can cause a person with mental illness who has been coping well to have problems. Sometimes a simple change like switching medication can be a problem.

I worked with a mother who was diagnosed with paranoid schizophrenia. Many people who hear this diagnosis assume that this mother could not possibly care for her children. But she was a good parent. She took medication regularly that controlled any problem symptoms. After several months of working with her, I noticed one day that she was confused and thinking slowly during a session. Knowing her history of mental illness, I asked whether she recently had a change in medication. It turned out that her doctor had just changed her prescription. She had not yet adjusted to the new medication.

Her ex-husband, who had known about her mental illness when he married her, agreed to a temporary change in their parenting arrangements. There was potential risk to the children with their mother's prescription change and the ex-husband had to travel out of town on business. We made arrangements for Grandma to stay with his ex-wife and their children for a few days. He also took the children for some extra time when he returned from his business trip. This gave his ex-wife time to get used to her new medication, while ensuring that the children were safe and well cared for.

Preparing for the Future

A "successful" divorce involves a gradual change from thinking of yourself as a husband or wife to thinking of yourself as a single parent. You step back emotionally from the marriage relationship and move into a coparent relationship. You and your ex are now coparents, not romantic partners.

We all change roles during our lives. We grow from being children to adults. We marry and become a husband or wife. We get promoted and become a supervisor. Our parents die and we become the person in the family everyone looks to for organizing family activities. Divorce, while painful, is just another role change. Stepping back to see it this way can make it a little easier to deal with. Not easy, but a little easier.

At the time of separation, you may find yourself acting in ways you never have before. You may cry easily, drink too much, have affairs, or get angry at the drop of a hat. You feel out of control. The world seems unfair. You wonder if life will ever be normal again.

The good news is, most people move out of this phase and back to more normal ways of dealing with life. Some people, however, get "stuck in chaos." The Parenting Coordinator may refer you for therapy if you are stuck and seem unable to move on with your life. You may need to learn new skills to deal with this period in your life. It's important that your children not be caught in the chaos with you. Children deserve a chance to grow in a secure environment and will be harmed if they are stuck in chaos with you and your ex. New research tells us that the way moms and dads parent plays a major role in how well children adjust both during the divorce and many years later.

Further, the *quality* of parenting is just as important as the way parents disentangle conflict. If you are angry or depressed or stressed out about money, for example, it is hard to have enough energy to have a positive attitude around your children, to be involved in their activities, and to be consistent in your discipline. Studies show that parents who are caught in high-conflict relationships with their ex are more likely to emotionally neglect their children and to use harsh or inconsistent forms of discipline.

The goal of parenting coordination is to help parents move to a cooperative way of solving problems as coparents. This gives the children a sense of their parents having a common purpose rather than being in a contest with each other. The contest happens because many divorcing parents are competitive. Each wants to win. Sometimes the need to win is at the expense of their children. The parents get locked in a struggle where the original issue (the children) is lost in a war of words and actions. Parents will often settle for a disaster rather than "losing." This way of thinking is *absolutely* toxic in raising children. The competitive style looks like this:

- Dishonesty and outright lying. False promises and misinformation may make it look as though cooperation is happening, but it is not. Parents can't trust what the other says.

- Suspicion of the other parent. This flows from the untrustworthy way that the other parent acted in the past. But now anything the other parent does is looked at with suspicion.

- Parents can't split up parenting tasks because they can't work together. As a result, balls get dropped (no one shows up at Pamela's choir concert because each thought the other was coming, and they did not want to both be there) or too many balls are thrown into the air at once (both parents arrive to pick up Parker from soccer practice because neither would trust that the other would follow the pickup schedule).

- Parents criticize and reject each other's ideas, even if the ideas are good ones.

Cooperative parenting—the goal of parenting coordination—looks very different. Parents share ideas, listen to each other, and consider each other's suggestions. Conversations are friendly and helpful. Parents don't throw up roadblocks to each other while working on problems. Parenting tasks are split up equally. Parents are willing to share power and control. Solutions to problems take into account everyone's needs—children, parents, and extended family.

Don't think that this process is all-or-nothing. You and your ex will not be in a heated conflict one day and then at peace the day after you meet with the Parenting Coordinator. It takes time. It is not all conflict or all cooperation. Rather, you and your coparent will be moving from conflict to cooperation, step by step. It gets easier as you learn to focus on the tasks of parenting, not the feelings of divorce.

As life moves on for you, your ex, and your children, you will continue to need to adapt to life's changes. This is a normal process for everyone, but for you it also means preparing for new parenting partners if you or your ex remarry, children who may come into the family by marriage or birth, new in-laws, and the changing needs of your children as they grow. Using cooperative parenting skills can help make this easier for everyone. Not easy, of course, as I have said before . . . just *easier*.

CHAPTER FIVE

Conflict, Change, and the Parenting Plan

Aiming at Conflict

This book has a lot of information about handling conflict because couples most often use parenting coordination during and after a divorce, when conflict is high. But you should know that conflict is not bad in and of itself. Any relationship will have some conflict in it, because people are not exactly alike. We are all different, wanting and needing different things. When those wants and needs are not the same, conflict can arise.

There are many different ways to deal with conflict, some better or worse than others. Most people find a way to deal with conflict and then move on. Not only is conflict normal and expected; conflict can be used as an opportunity to learn different ways of thinking and behaving. Conflict can be a way to grow as a parent and as a relationship partner.

But some people cannot seem to let go of conflict. They hold on to the conflict even though it is painful and damaging to everyone involved. In this case, the only lesson being learned is what frustration and anger feel like. The Parenting Coordinator is brought in to *analyze* the conflict, *identify* solutions, and help the parents *manage* conflict. This has a handy acronym: AIM.

This AIM process is intended to open up possibilities for solving problems that parents, locked in conflict, may not have been able to see. The way to begin this process is to identify each parent's "interests." We talked about this in an earlier chapter: interests are basic ideas such as "I believe our children should be law-abiding citizens." If the parents agree on these basic ideas, it is much easier to solve conflict.

In high-conflict divorces, it often feels as if the conflict itself is all that is left between the two of you, forgetting that you have common goals for your children or at least a common desire NOT to harm the children. But knowing that some conflict is part of any relationship can help change the way you think about it. If you think about conflict as only one part of a long-term relationship, it helps put the relationship in a different light. This does not mean that the process is quick and easy. You have likely been in conflict so long that both you and your coparent have some bad habits to break. You may find yourself automatically getting angry when your ex brings up an idea, without listening for the "interest" in the idea first. What will the idea mean for your children? The Parenting Coordinator can help you and your coparent learn new ways of thinking. In this way, you can both move on and create a new family system that allows your children to thrive.

Conflict can often be changed into something positive. When this is not possible, it can, at the very least, be *contained*. Think about what happens when there is a bad accident on the highway: the police block off lanes of traffic to prevent other cars from driving through broken glass or spilled gas. Conflict can be contained in much the same way to keep your children away from dangerous areas.

In analyzing the conflict, the Parenting Coordinator may ask questions to understand how it started and why it has continued. The Parenting Coordinator may also ask about the way you dealt with conflict before the divorce. Sometimes, the legal system itself causes conflict to continue. If parents cannot make a decision together about their children, then the judge listens to each parent's side and makes the decision. If the judge's decision is closer to what Dad wants, then he is likely to feel like a "winner" and Mom may feel like a "loser." This means parents may see themselves in competition, instead of cooperating for the good of their children. Studies have shown that competing for a win does not result in a good agreement for parenting.

A better way to resolve conflict is to identify interests (what do you want for your children), separate the person from the problem (this is not about your ex; it is about dental visits for Parker), think of several options (be creative in coming up with possible solutions), and make an agreement that is based on facts, not feelings (Parker needs two dental visits per year, fact). In my practice, I often use a flip chart to list the conflict, brainstorm options, and write out the solution. This helps to take the edge off the highly charged feelings around the conflict. The flip chart is, after all, a business tool. The business here is parenting children.

Be Creative

The Parenting Coordinator is not the only person responsible for being creative in thinking of solutions. You and your coparent are full of creative ideas. The problem is, conflict has made it hard to be creative. It is too easy to slip back into the "I am right, he is wrong" mind-set. It takes some effort to pull away from right and wrong and focus instead on what is *best* for your children. The parenting coordination process can be hard work, especially at first. Breaking old habits is not easy. Nor is it easy to learn new ways of thinking. The good news is that it gets easier with practice. What seemed impossible at first can be done with some effort. Then it can be done a little bit easier. After more practice, what seemed impossible is now a new way of thinking and being. When you look back, you will be amazed at the changes you and your ex have made. Better yet, you will be pleased with the positive changes in your children as you and your coparent create a good plan for parenting your children.

It is important to be realistic about the work involved in the business of parenting. Good parents do not just "happen." Good parents are always thinking of the best interests of their children. What is best for the children will not always be the same. Children change. The family changes. The economy gets worse and there is less money in the family. A family member moves away or dies. Good parents are constantly changing how they parent based on what is going on at the time. Things cannot stay the same—and should not stay the same. Some parents tell me, "Oh, I wish it could just be the same as it was." But it can't ever be the same. Nor should it be the same. Even if everything were perfect, parenting would change with time because children grow and change.

Some parents, wishing for "and they all lived happily ever after" think change itself is bad. However, it's easier to cope with life, as it flows by from day to day, when you view change as expected and normal. In fact, change can be better for everyone, as in this example:

John got a new job that paid a lot more but required travel. He couldn't always predict when he would need to travel, which was a problem for the parenting plan. Shelly's first reaction was to hold John to their schedule without any exceptions. He would just lose visit time if he were traveling when normally scheduled to be with the children.

John's interests: *to have healthy, happy children*
                          to make more money to support the family
                          to have quality time with his children

Shelly's interests: *to have healthy, happy children*
                          to have more time with the children
                          to have time and money to pamper herself a little

In talking about this conflict, Shelly had trouble at first seeing why she should change the parenting schedule. After all, she would get to have John's parenting time added to her time with the children, meeting one of her interests. When the couple was asked to think creatively, however, they found a new way of thinking about the situation.

John's extra pay means child support payments could be increased.

Shelly could use the extra money to cut down on the hours she works.

Shelly gets extra time with the children.

Shelly can be flexible with John's parenting schedule because they both will get what they want.

Where Are We?

Conflict has a cycle, just as there are seasons in our year. It can be helpful to know where you and your ex are on the conflict cycle. You may be on the uphill curve, with conflict getting worse and worse. Or you may be at a point where you are stuck, hurting and hopeless, in endless conflict. Parenting coordination works to move you and your ex "over the hump" toward dispute settlement and peace building.

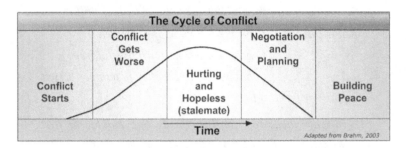

This graph looks very neat and clean, doesn't it? But we all know that people don't behave in such neat and orderly ways. Parents may bounce back and forth in the cycle, or be doing very well for a long time until something new comes up to trigger conflict again. This can happen, for example, when your ex decides to remarry. A new parent (the stepparent) has been thrown into the equation. Now your ex may be paying more attention to his new partner instead of your children. Or the new partner may upset the parenting plan with demands of her own.

The other problem with this neat, clean graph is that it is very easy for one parent to point out how their coparent needs to change in order to resolve conflict. "If my ex would just see it my way, everything would be fine" sounds good when *you* say it but not when your ex is saying it to you. It is much easier to blame your ex than look at what *you* may be doing that keeps the conflict going.

Here we get into another cycle problem. It is the cycle of blame-defense-anger. In this cycle, one parent drags up an incident that proves what is wrong with the other person and why he or she can't be trusted. Then the other person does the same. Each move in the cycle of blame and resentment points a finger at the other person as being responsible for what is going on. The conflict gets worse by the minute, and whatever goodwill may have been built quickly fades away. And, worse still, the cycle of blame-defense-anger then starts all over again.

The Parenting Coordinator helps parents understand the concept of goodwill. According to this concept, each parent makes goodwill "deposits" (doing or saying something positive) but also can make goodwill "withdrawals" (doing or saying something hurtful). For most high-conflict parents, their goodwill bank account is seriously in the red when they begin the parenting coordination process. Here are some questions to help slow or stop this cycle:

- How did this vicious cycle start to take over?
- How did it catch you both in its patterns against your better judgment?
- How did you get swept along in the wake of this conflict?
- What would be your guess about how much blame is in charge of your views of each other?
- To what extent is blame stopping you from resolving your differences?
- How much are you in charge rather than letting blame have things its own way?

The most targeted question is about choice: "Are you planning to allow the conflict to continue to speak for you and direct your behavior?"

Zoom In, Zoom Out

On a GPS, you can touch the screen to zoom in and get a closer look at where you are going. You can see in large print or graphics the next crossroad. You may even see what lane to be in and which lanes to avoid. Then, you can touch the screen to zoom out to get the big picture. This is what the Parenting Coordinator helps you and your coparent do when you are locked in conflict.

What is the big picture? It is the health and well-being of your children. From a distance, the things you were arguing about appear small, minimized by the height you are seeing them from. Sometimes just getting that distance is all it takes. Some parents hate each other so much that all they can think about is getting even—hurting the other person as much as possible. When this happens, the conflict is zoomed in to the maximum. Neither parent sees anything but the other parent. These parents may be separated physically, but emotionally they are stuck together.

Imagine what would happen if you were driving down the road looking only at the person in your vehicle's passenger's seat. How long do you suppose it would be before you ran into something or someone? That kind of car wreck is what happens to your children. While you and your ex are staring each other down, the car crashes and your children are hurt.

This is not to say that real damage has not been done to each other in the past. Your ex may still be trying to hurt you while you are trying to move on with the important business of raising your children and establishing a new, happy life for yourself. For example, your ex may flaunt her relationship with the man she had the affair with when you were still married. Or she may tell relatives and friends unflattering stories of your failures in the past.

One way that a Parenting Coordinator might zoom out is to make the problem . . . the problem. For instance, "So, the conflict has gotten you to feel a very intense feeling like hatred. How did it manage to take over your feelings in such a strong way?" Or, "How did this argument catch you both in its clutches?" This approach reduces the sense of blame and invites parents to look at the conflict as some*thing*, not some*one*. In other words, the problem is not the other person, but rather, the problem is the problem. The conflict has been turned into a fact, which can open possibilities for new ways of thinking.

It is important for parents to separate the issues in conflict from the person with whom they are in conflict. Blame can be woven so tightly around the parents in a conflict that they have a hard time setting aside negative feelings to talk about the issues. The Parenting Coordinator may remind the parents that, when they discipline a child, they focus on the unacceptable behavior of the child. They don't label the child herself as "bad." It's the behavior that is the problem, not the child.

When conflict has gone on for a long time, some parents have a habit of automatically thinking the other parent's feelings, wishes, or ideas are unreasonable or labeling them as "stupid." The Parenting Coordinator can point this out: "I know

Role	What They Say
Teacher	"Here's another way." "This information may be helpful."
Facilitator	"What is needed here?"
Bridge Builder	"I'd like to introduce you to . . . (a therapist, educator, etc.)."
Mediator	"Let's work this out."
Arbitrator	"What's fair here is . . ."
Equalizer	"Let's level the playing field."
Healer	"Let's make amends."
Witness	"Look what's happening!"
Referee	"No throwing things!"
Peacekeeper	"Break it up!"

you may not think Marie's feelings are important or reasonable, but everyone is entitled to their own feelings. Feelings aren't right or wrong. Let's see if we can understand what's behind

Marie's feelings, so we can move forward in resolving the conflicts between you that are affecting your children."

Intense conflict can get ugly. Sometimes it just gets to be too much. Your ex has said so many hurtful things, one after the other, that you just lose it. Parenting coordinators call this *flooding*, where a person feels overwhelmed by the way the other person is communicating. When people experience emotional flooding, their body is a confused jumble of signals. Their muscles tense and stay tensed, their heart beats faster, and they may find it hard to breathe. This makes it hard to listen, think, and understand what it going on. The flood has swept away coping skills in a wash of feelings.

When this happens, a Parenting Coordinator will call it out. The Parenting Coordinator may say, for instance, "I think we are off the subject," "I think we have lost our focus on the children and the goal," "Your comment was aggressive and will not help us move forward," or "I don't think listening is occurring between the two of you." I keep a yellow referee flag—the kind used in football to call a penalty—for just these situations. I stand up and throw the penalty flag on the floor between the two parents. "Penalty!" I will say, loudly. "Not listening to each other!"

Through working with a Parenting Coordinator, parents learn how to identify their conflict so they can focus on problem-solving. For example, a parent who calls the coparent a "selfish jerk" is not identifying a parenting problem. She is name-calling. But if the parent notes that her ex tends to think of his own needs before the needs of their children, that is a specific behavior that can be worked on. Consider this example:

Bill: "I want to pick Parker up at 8 p.m. on Friday nights so

I can stop after work and have a few beers with the guys."

Eve: "Parker's football games start at 7 p.m. and he has asked that you come see him play, then take him home. Parker first." ("Parker first" is a phrase this couple uses to remind themselves to think of the children first)

Bill: "Oh, right . . . Okay, I can get there by 7."

Another strategy is to look at the effects conflict has had on each parent and their children. Think about these questions:

- What effects would you say distrust has had on your ability to coparent?
- What has this ongoing conflict cost you?
- Are there ways in which this conflict has gotten you to act out of character?
- Has this conflict made you more effective or less effective as a parent?
- What impact has this conflict had on your personal life, your business, your relationships, your performance at work, your rest and relaxation, your confidence, your attitudes, your beliefs, your bank balance?

Now think about the conflict going on and on . . . and on. Then ask yourself this question:

- "What will happen if the conflicts between you go on for three months, six months, one year, two years, five years . . . ten years?"

If you are zoomed in to the conflict and can see only the conflict, it can be very helpful to zoom out and think ahead. What would life be like with the conflict? And, what would it be like without the conflict?

I'm Right and You're Wrong

The hardest conflicts to resolve are those based on what the parents see as moral issues. These are often seen as black and white, or as right or wrong. No compromise can be imagined. Parents can get stuck when they cannot see any way around one of these issues.

As an example of a moral issue causing a conflict, let's consider a family I worked with several years ago. The mother had converted to Judaism after the wedding. The couple's two children were raised Jewish. After the divorce, the wife went back to her original faith, attending the Roman Catholic Church regularly. The parents became locked in conflict over the issue of religion. Mom insisted on the children attending weekly Mass with Communion as well as attending catechism classes. Dad insisted the children attend Hebrew school and synagogue.

Differences in religious beliefs have led to wars between nations. It is no wonder that religion can cause war in a divorce. In the situation above, I worked with the parents to identify their interests: Dad wanted the boys to celebrate their Bar Mitzvah (which occurs around age thirteen) and to understand his family's Jewish heritage and religion. Mom wanted the children to be exposed to her religious beliefs and participate in religious services with her. Since the children were eight and ten when their parents divorced, they were still forming their own ideas about religion. So the parents agreed that the children would be exposed to *both* religious beliefs. Mom agreed to attend a church where they could celebrate mass on Saturday afternoons when they were with her. Dad agreed the he would take the children to temple on Friday evenings when they were with him. Since Hebrew training, a precursor to becoming a Bar Mitzvah, occurred on Sunday mornings, the parents agreed that Dad would take each child for this training every week for one year prior to the Bar Mitzvah. The parents agreed that they would plan the Bar Mitzvah celebration together and after the celebration, the children were free to choose the religious services they wanted to attend.

A person's sense of fairness and justice can also lead to conflict. Our sense of justice is linked to the rights we believe we are owed. Being denied what we are owed, or not being treated in a fair manner, can lead to a stubborn refusal to back down. Financial issues in the settlement are often matters of fairness. When one party spends down resources before the divorce, or tries not to pay alimony or child support, things can get very ugly, very quickly.

The problem is that justice is not always black and white. What one person thinks is fair, another will think is completely unacceptable. One way to work out these problems is to consult some independent standard of fairness. Sometimes this is the court. Sometimes the Parenting Coordinator can show parents research by scientists that helps defuse the conflict. There are also times when the Parenting Coordinator may be able to show parents how their conflict is affecting their children. The parents may have been so focused on each other that they didn't realize the effect on their children. The Parenting Coordinator may also take on a role to help solve the conflict. These roles may include teacher, facilitator, bridge builder, and referee, amongst others.

Conflict that has reached a stalemate can be seen as a plateau, a flat area that goes on and on. But at the end of the plateau is a cliff—a place where both parents know that things will suddenly get much worse. If both parents see a cliff approaching, they are more likely to look for a solution. This can happen when increasing legal fees are steadily eating up all of the parents' money. It can also happen when the conflict leads to a crisis with their children.

I worked with a family where parents had been in conflict for over five years. The couple's twelve-year-old son made a "mock" suicide video and posted it on a social media website. Several family members saw the video and showed it to the parents. This was a very real cliff: their son was so upset with their endless conflict that he was thinking of killing himself. The parents were shocked and scared enough to try to work things out and end the conflict. The problem was, they had been in conflict for so long they didn't know how to change. It took parenting coordination to show them a different way to relate to each other.

> **Tip:** Remember that interests can be compatible even when positions are not.

Recalculating

You are driving and try a new route. The road stops at a dead end. The GPS voice says, "Recalculating." In a moment, it gives you a new direction.

There are times when parents cannot resolve their conflict, even by looking at their interests rather than their positions. At these times the Parenting Coordinator must, like the GPS, recalculate. A new plan must be made to contain the conflict and keep the children safe. Parents are taught to keep their conflict within certain bounds and limit its intensity. Think of Switzerland and you get the idea. Switzerland is a neutral country that does not go to war.

Recalculating happens at other times, too. Your children may lose their way. You may lose your focus in the parenting plan. And the unexpected will always crop up. In all of these instances, the plan must be tweaked in order to get your children back on track. Ongoing "checkup" meetings with the Parenting Coordinator will monitor the status of the parenting plan. Sometimes the recalculation is needed because the family is changing in ways no one expected. Or an expected change happened sooner than planned. Whatever the changes, the Parenting Coordinator helps modify the parenting plan as needed.

Tips for Resolving Conflict

- Think outside the box.
- Don't think "win/lose."
- Find what works.
- Talk about the children's needs, not yours.

An example of recalculation happened with a family who had a twelve-year-old son. His teachers suggested that he might have attention deficit disorder (ADD). The father did not want his son on medication and labeled his son's behavior as "normal guy stuff." The mother was worried about the child's poor grades in school and increase in problem behavior at home and school. The parents were in a stalemate; both thought their position was the right one. The Parenting Coordinator suggested that the parents agree to gather independent information from a number of different professionals to help them with this problem.

They agreed to consult a child psychiatrist, a psychologist who specialized in ADD, and an educator and split the costs.

Gathering data helped reframe the conflict from one that was positional (it's either *right* or *wrong* to use medication) to a study of facts gleaned from outside professionals. The parents agreed to meet with each professional separately before having the professional meet with their son. This took away any worry about bias ("The psychologist just said what you wanted him to say"). The parents also agreed to write up a list of their interests for the other parent to read and comment on.

When the professional evaluations were complete, the Parenting Coordinator gathered the reports and reviewed them with the parents. They discussed options and possible outcomes for their son—as facts, not as emotional positions. The parents were able to reach an agreement to have the child take medication for six weeks. They made a list of specific things to track during this time—behavior, grades, and so on. Then their son would be taken off the medications for six weeks, again tracking behavior and grades. Afterward, the parents compared the two trial periods to help them make a logical decision based on how the medication affected their son—not how they felt about their son taking medication for ADD.

CHAPTER SIX

Selecting Your Plan

A Customized Plan

No two families are exactly alike. No two children are exactly alike, either, even identical twins. Every child, and every family, has its own unique flavor. Plans that work for one family may not work for another family. That is why parenting plans are not "cookie-cutter" plans.

In a book like this, I cannot set a standard or even an ideal parenting plan that will fit every family. This book also can't offer customized recommendations for every family. The information in this chapter (and the book as a whole) is intended to help you think, reflect, discuss, plan, and then develop a parenting plan for your children's healthy future. *This assessment is just a tool for planning. It is not intended to be used as evidence in court.*

You can continue to use this information as a reference as your children grow and your situation changes. I encourage you to review your parenting plans as your children reach new developmental stages as well as when significant events such as remarriage and relocation are planned.

Keys to Success
- Be honest in looking at your family's needs.
- Focus on the needs of your children.

Now, here is the legal disclaimer: The self-assessment and sample parenting plans provided in this chapter are offered as a guide. They were developed by a group (of which I was a member) for the Twelfth Judicial Circuit in Florida. Legal matters can be very complex. If you have questions or concerns about the use of these forms, instructions, or your legal rights, it is strongly recommended that you talk to an attorney. Neither I nor the Twelfth Judicial Circuit guarantee that these forms or instructions will get the results you want. It's also not possible to guarantee that your coparent (or children, or family members) will follow the plan. The judge in your case may not follow the plan you create exactly. Use this information at your own risk; neither the Twelfth Judicial Circuit nor I will be responsible for any losses incurred by any person in reliance on the instructions and/or forms.

Now that that's out of the way, we can start with the self-assessment tools for you and your family. You can see the types of questions asked in the self-assessment tools, and also go online to download and print them at: http://www.thencpc.com/.

Start on the next page for the first steps in designing the plan. Answer the self-assessment questions that are laid out in steps. Be honest with yourself as you answer all of the questions in this section. Honest answers will lead to the best parenting plan for your children. Although all of the self-assessment questions are listed on the following pages, you may find it most helpful to download and print the forms.

Designing the Plan

The next step is designing the plan, which calls for several assessments of the family. The following pages list the factors considered in the plan. You may access the form online at: www.thencpc.com/services/parents-families/parenting-plans.html

STEP ONE: FAMILY ASSESSMENT

Answer "Yes" or "No":

Has the other parent:

1. Acted as though violent behavior against you or your child(ren) is all right?

2. Damaged or destroyed property during an argument?

3. Hurt a pet out of anger?

4. Been so sad or upset they could not care for themselves or others?

5. Pushed, slapped, kicked, punched, or hit you or the child(ren)?

6. Regularly abused and currently abuses alcohol and/or drugs?

7. Used weapons to threaten or hurt people?

8. Threatened to never return the child(ren)?

9. Threatened to kill you or the child(ren)?

10. Sexually abused anyone by force, threat of force, or intimidation?

11. Been served with a protection or no contact order?

12. Been arrested for harming or threatening to harm you or anyone else?

13. Engaged in any other abusive or threatening behavior?

If you answered "Yes" to one or more of the above questions, you may need a Safety Focused Plan. You can access a sample plan at: /www.thencpc.com/services/parents-families/parenting-plans.html.

If you answered "No" to all of these questions, please continue with the next step.

STEP TWO: HIGHLY STRUCTURED ASSESSMENT

Answer "Yes" or "No":

1. I only communicate with my child's other parent by using email, certified U.S. mail, a third party (lawyer, relative, faith-based professional, etc.), our child(ren). (Don't answer "Yes" if simply living far apart causes this.)

2. I do not believe my child(ren)'s other parent is a good parent.

3. I do not trust my child(ren)'s other parent to consistently use good judgment and make good decisions regarding our child.

4. I keep written and/or recorded records of all contact between myself and my child(ren)'s other parent.

5. I feel it is okay to make all major decisions about my child(ren) without consulting the other parent, because I have our child(ren)'s best interest at heart.

6. My child(ren)'s other parent and I can only exchange our child(ren) in a public setting, with an adult third party present with the police present, and/or by maintaining a safe physical distance.

7. Because of the actions of my child(ren)'s other parent, I have serious concerns regarding our child(ren)'s emotional and psychological functioning, peer or social relations, mother/

child(ren) relationship, father/child(ren) relationship, school performance, behavior, and/or physical health.

Note: The taping or recording of others without their consent is usually illegal.

If you answered "Yes" to one or more of the above questions, you may need a Highly Structured Parenting Plan. You may access the form online at: www.thencpc.com/services/parents-families/parenting-plans.html

If you answered "No" to all of these questions, please continue with the next step.

STEP THREE: DISTANCE ASSESSMENT

- Do you and the other parent live or plan to live more than fifty miles apart? Is it unlikely that you will have much contact with each other?

If the answer is "Yes," you may need a Long-Distance Parenting Plan.

You may access the form online at: www.thencpc.com/services/parents-families/parenting-plans.html

If you answered "No," please continue.

STEP FOUR: SELF-ASSESSMENT

DAILY SCHEDULE

- If you are employed outside the home:
  What time do you leave? What time do you return?
- If employed in the home, do you need to be home certain hours? Can your schedule be changed?
- Are there any demands on your time after normal work hours?

- Is out-of-town travel required? If yes, how often? How long are you gone?

OUTSIDE HELP

- Do you have any additional help from other family or friends to care for your child(ren)? Are you a caregiver for anyone other than your child(ren)?

TRANSPORTATION

- Do you have reliable transportation?
- Do you have a valid driver's license?
- Do you have any health issues that might affect your ability to drive?

PARENTING

- In what events or situations do(es) the child(ren):
  Ask you for help?
  Respond to your direction?
  Not respond to your direction?
- What do you do well as a parent?
- What do you have trouble with as a parent?

COMMUNICATION

- Do you have problems communicating with the other parent?
- Do you have email access?
  Internet access?
  Cell/Smart phone?
  Text messaging?

FAMILY EVENTS

- What events or holidays are the most important to you?

DISCIPLINE

- What kind of discipline do you use?
- What kind works for your child(ren)?

STEP FIVE: COPARENT ASSESSMENT

DAILY SCHEDULE

- If the other parent is employed outside the home: What time does the parent leave? What time does the parent return?
- If the other parent is employed in the home, does he or she need to be home certain hours?
  Can his or her schedule be changed?
- Are there any demands on the other parent's time after normal work hours?
- Is out-of-town travel required?
- If yes, how often? How long is the parent gone?

OUTSIDE HELP

- Does the other parent have additional help from other family or friends?
- Is this parent a caregiver for anyone other than your child(ren)?

TRANSPORTATION

- Does the other parent have reliable transportation?
- Does the other parent have a valid driver's license?
- Does the other parent have any health issues that might affect his or her ability to drive?

PARENTING

- In what events or situations do(es) the child(ren):
  Ask for the other parent's help?
  Respond to the other parent's direction?
  Not respond to the other parent's direction?
- What does the other parent do well as a parent?
- What does the other parent have trouble with as a parent?

COMMUNICATION

- Does the other parent have problems communicating with you?
- Does the other parent have e-mail access?
  Internet access?
  Cell/Smart phone?
  Text messaging?

FAMILY EVENTS

- What events or holidays are important to the other parent?

DISCIPLINE

- What kind of discipline does the other parent use?
- What kind works for your child(ren)?

STEP SIX: CHILD ASSESSMENT

In this section you will assess your child. Complete one assessment per child if you have more than one child. Be honest with yourself about what is working now—and what isn't. Parenting after a divorce is never the same. Be aware that one parent may not have been an active parent before the divorce or may have pulled back from parenting during a separation. Either parent may want to become a more active parent now.

The parenting plan should allow time for that parent to develop or redevelop a closer relationship with your children.

- What is the child's age? School? Grade?
- Is the child emotionally closer to one parent than the other? If yes, which one?
- Has the child experienced any traumatic separations or deaths? If yes, when and what?
- Has the child ever been diagnosed by a licensed professional with any academic needs, physical problems, or emotional disorders?
- Who was the child evaluated by? Diagnosis? When diagnosed? Treatment plan?
- Has this child changed schools other than for normal progression? Or been held back a grade?
- Skipped a grade in school?
- Had difficulty in school?
- Been provided an Individualized Educational Plan (IEP)?
- Been found to be academically gifted?
- Does the child have special needs?
- How long is the travel time from your: home, work, child's school, tutors, sporting activities, pediatrician, extracurricular activities, place of worship?
- How long is the travel time from: the other parent's home, the other parent's work, child's school, tutors, sporting activities, pediatrician, extracurricular activities, place of worship.
- Does the child currently participate in any activities? On what days of the week?

- Do you have any future planned activities?
- How do you and this child spend time together? When?

Now that you have completed the Self Assessment and decided which plan is likely to be most useful for your family, you are ready to start mapping out a strategy to develop an effective and sustainable plan for you and your coparent.

Important Factors to Remember in Creating Parenting Plans

Minimize loss: For children, divorce is about loss. The separation and divorce of their parents means losing home, family life, loving parents who care about each other, pets, financial security, familiar schools, friends, and a daily routine.

Maximize relationships: Encourage all relationships the children had before the separation (with parents, grandparents, aunts, uncles, friends, and so on). Your children will continue to feel connected to family when they have pleasant, free access to both parents and both extended families. Your children's identity depends on their feeling they belong to both families. If possible, share the responsibilities (doctors' appointments, transportation) and the joyous events (holidays, movies, birthday parties) equally with the other parent.

Protect your child's feelings: Children need to hear that they are not responsible for the separation. However, try to avoid blaming the other parent for the separation, as this forces children to "take sides." Let your children be children: don't confide in them or share details of adult relationships. Children may say that they don't mind listening, but they may later feel confused and resentful. Children are harmed when they hear one parent say bad things about the other parent.

Increase security: Scientific research confirms that children will suffer now and later if they frequently see their parents in conflict. Raised voices, arguing, hateful remarks, and physical fights are not good for your children to see or hear. Do not discuss adult issues at the time of transfers or at other times when the child is present.

Age-related needs: Children of different ages need and benefit from different parenting arrangements. Parents should try to be flexible, tailoring schedules as much as possible to reflect their child's developmental needs. Expect to be more flexible as your child gets older. It is just a fact of life that life gets more complicated as children grow older—more activities, more friends, just more going on overall.

In any parenting plan, it is important to remember that children develop best when both parents have meaningful and stable involvement in their children's lives. Each parent has a different and valuable contribution to make to the children's development.

For younger children especially, it is better that they spend more time with parents and less time with other caregivers, if possible.

Communication and cooperation between parents is important. Not always easy, but important. Having consistent rules in both households and sharing knowledge of events creates a sense of security for children of all ages. Households must discuss and plan school activities and other events.

If children are allowed to bring their personal items back and forth between the households, they develop a better sense of ownership and responsibility. Parents should purchase special things for the children but not merely for their own household.

Review and possibly revise the parenting plan at these points:

- A child starts school
- A child's schedule changes
- A parent remarries
- Any family member experiences any major change

The Do's and Don'ts of Parenting

This section includes tips for parents in "do" and "don't" categories. These tips are taken from research on the most effective parenting for children of divorce, as well as from my many years of experience working with families.

Both Parents

DO

- Maintain healthy communication with your children.
- Make it a priority to communicate regularly with the other parent.
- Follow the parenting plan to make the process routine, easy, and positive for your children.
- Try to keep your word to the children. Don't make promises you can't keep.
- Contact the other parent immediately if there is an emergency involving the children while they are with you.

DON'T

- Be uncooperative. The children will suffer consequences if their parents do not cooperate.

Parent A
(The parent who may have more parenting time)

DO

- Share information about school, teachers, activities, friends, and relatives with the other parent.

- Be flexible and supportive of the children's relationship with the other parent. "I think it's great that you and your mom are getting along so well."

- Encourage excitement for the anticipated communication and/or travel with the other parent. "This weekend with your dad should be fun. Enjoy the fishing trip."

DON'T

- Edit, coach, monitor, or otherwise interfere with the children's communication with the other parent.

- Take it personally if the children do not wish to call you regularly when they are with the other parent.

Parent B
(The parent who may have less parenting time)

DO

- Make an extra effort to initiate contact with the children. Learn about their daily activities. "Tell me about your new teacher. What is she like?".

- Provide an itinerary to the other parent to prepare the children for the visit. Let the other parent know what activities you are planning. "Here is the schedule for the kids' visit. We will be going to the zoo Saturday and to church on Sunday. They will need outdoor clothes and church clothes."

- Always try to keep your word to the children. "I can't promise to be at your game Thursday night because of work. But I can promise to be at the game on Saturday."

DON'T

- Take it personally if the children do not wish to stay on the phone too long or do not call right back.

- Unreasonably limit the children's contact with the local parent during their stay.

Sample Parenting Plans

Now that you've completed the self-assessments, you may have a better idea of which parenting plan is right for you. In this chapter, you were referred to several sample parenting plans on The National Cooperative Parenting Center website. Remember that these are only samples. Your parenting plan will undoubtedly need customization to fit your children's needs and the legal requirements for the area where you live.

If the courts in your area do not use or require a parenting plan, then you can use this as a guide with your mediator and with your coparent. Use these plans as templates, and add to them as needed. The following Parenting Plans can be accessed at www.TheNCPC.com or by calling 1-888-455-NCPC (6272).

1. Basic Parenting Plan
2. Distance Parenting Plan
3. Structured Parenting Plan
4. Safety Parenting Plan

CHAPTER SEVEN

Bumps in the Road

When the parenting road gets bumpy, it can be hard to stick to the parenting plan. Sometimes the bumps are of your own making. Old hurts and resentment get in the way. Just this once, you would like to tell your children about the pain your ex has put you through. Money is tight and there is less time than ever to get everything done. And then . . . one of your children takes a street drug a friend gives her. Or your ex starts drinking again. Or your ex threatens to hurt your new boyfriend. The road is rough ahead. Hang on tight. It's time to problem solve.

The best way to handle the bumps in the road is to be prepared. This is not as hard as it sounds. Not all bumps are surprises. For example, you know that as children move through developmental stages there will be bumps. If you pay attention to your children's behavior and match it with developmental stages, you will be ready when your child "suddenly" wants to be with friends more than with you and the family.

You can also watch for signs of upcoming problems. A small bit of extra attention can prevent a huge amount of fixing. I often tell parents to "recognize thunder when you hear it in the distance." Here are some examples:

Pamela comes home from a date with a hickey on her neck. (It's time to talk about sexual boundaries, if you haven't done this already.)

Parker and his friend Jim were at the house studying while you were at work yesterday. You notice that the bottle of vodka is almost empty. (Is Parker drinking with his friend? Ask him directly.)

Pamela's grades are starting to slip—not a lot, but her grades are lower in two classes this semester. (Check on Pamela's study habits, use a checklist system for homework, and talk to her teachers.)

Some of you who are reading this are likely thinking, "But why don't I just wait and see if something bad happens? Why jump in so soon?" The waiting strategy does work sometimes. Some things don't grow into problems or they just go away on their own. But many of them don't. When you wait and see, you run the risk of the problem growing so large you can't fix it. The difficulty is, it's hard to tell the difference between the issue that will resolve itself with time and the issue that needs to be dealt with—now. Add to that what feels like a lack of resources ("I don't have time for this") and it is so easy to just sidestep the problem and . . . wait and see what happens.

Some people approach problems with the idea that they will use the quickest, easiest fix they can find. This is called the "Band-Aid" solution, and it works sometimes. However, getting into the habit of a quick-fix means you can resolve the surface problem while letting the real problem get worse and worse.

Most Parenting Coordinators spend a lot of time helping parents identify the true source of conflict and working out solutions. Learning to solve problems is a skill that can be used in most areas of life: communicating with your ex, parenting your children, working with other employees, volunteering for the Parent-Teacher Organization, or even leading a book group. Because life is all about people interacting with people, there will always be problems. This is a guarantee. Learning to spot problems early, and then to fix them, is an invaluable skill. Your divorce may actually lead to some helpful growth in other areas of your life. The skills you learn become second nature, and you will begin to use them every day.

Letting Go

One of the bumps in the road that I often see in my practice is *letting go*. Interestingly, this can take two opposite forms. One is the parent who is still romantically attached to the other parent. The couple may be divorced, but one parent still has secret (or even not-so-secret) dreams that they will get back together or at least she shouldn't be with another partner. The other way not letting go is a problem is in the parent who holds on to past hurts and resentments. These problems seem to be unrelated, but they both have to do with a parent not letting go, either of positive or negative feelings.

The parent who hangs on to the hope of getting back together doesn't want to let go of memories of good times and the hope of a happy future. This parent can't imagine how to make a happy life without the ex. It's easier to think that the past can come back. Moving on is painful. It means admitting the marriage failed. This logically leads to the idea that the parent failed. After all, if she were a better wife, would he have had an affair? Or if he was a better husband, would she have told him she was bored in the marriage and wanted out?

At the other end of the spectrum is the parent who holds

on to past hurts. This parent has a long list of hurtful actions the ex has done. The list is taken out and recalled often. Nothing is forgotten. Nothing is forgiven. This parent is living on a diet of anger and resentment. You may think that the hurts are exaggerated, or even made up. But much of the time these are very real hurts. Because the focus is on the ex, it is hard to move on. The focus is backward, toward the past. It's hard to see the road ahead when looking behind.

Both of these parent types need to let go, but doing so will not be easy for either. One has to give up dreams of the future, and one has to give up the nightmare of the past. Both need to look ahead, for their children's sake. This can "clean the windshield" through which they look at themselves, their ex, and the parenting issues before them.

Letting go means you are no longer working on getting even or getting back together with your ex. Some parents have to let go of the idea that their ex will be made to pay for what he has done. Payback can be emotional or monetary. Letting go of the idea of payback is hard for many parents.

I will mention forgiveness again as a way for parents to move on. Think of forgiveness as a way to gain a sense of control, predictability, and safety in your relationship with your ex. Forgiveness is not saying that your ex is not "guilty as charged" of the harsh things that have been done. It's about your wish to move on with your life and not continue to spend time, energy, and financial resources to stay where you are.

Too Far/Too Close

Another bump in the road is a parent who has closeness problems: too far away or too close. The "faraway" parent is one who is not very interested in being a parent. The "too close" parent is one who is more interested in children as friends than in children who must be parented. Both of these parent behaviors are bumps in the road because they get in the way of the children's healthy growth.

Parents who are not very interested in being a parent may be wrapped up in their own interests. Raising children takes time and effort. They may be so involved in a new romantic relationship that they are not paying attention to the parenting plan. Or they may take shortcuts with the plan: "I didn't take Parker to the tutor today. I just let him read his geography book. That's enough for him." Some parents go so far as lying about what was or wasn't done. These parents may even ask the children to lie for them. "Tell Dad I took you to the tutor today, Parker. I'll buy you the new game you've been wanting."

The Parenting Coordinator work with the faraway parent to set common interests and then to verify that the parenting plan is being followed. The Parenting Coordinator is not a judge but can check "evidence" to confirm that the parenting plan is being followed.

It would seem that parents who are very close to their children are good parents. "Mom is my best friend," eight-year-old Pamela says. "She lets me stay up late to watch TV with her in her bed. We eat popcorn together. We don't mind that Dad isn't home anymore." While Pamela may think having a mother for a best friend is a good thing, it is not healthy for Pamela or for her mother. Children need a parent to set rules and boundaries. Parents can become friends with their children after they are grown and living outside the home.

The stress of a divorce may leave a parent longing for a friend to confide in. After a divorce, the extra time needed to juggle work, child care, housework, paying bills, and all the other needs of daily life often leave little time for friendship. It is tempting to use your children in this role, especially if the child is a teenager. "Jessica is sixteen. She's old enough for me to talk to about how I feel." The problem is, Jessica is not old enough to have her mother switch places with her. Jessica needs to concentrate on being a teenager—not an easy thing to do. She needs a parent who will be a parent, setting limits and giving information about her changing body and emotional relationships. She needs Too Close to become, like Goldilocks, Just Right.

Mental Illness

> *"Hello, Mrs. Smith? This is David. I am a social worker at Valley View Psychiatric Hospital. Your ex-husband asked me to call you. I understand that the two of you have joint custody of your children. He has been admitted for a few days and we would like you to meet with you so that you can understand your husband's diagnosis and how to work with him as a coparent now that he is on medication."*

Mental illness can be a scary bump in the road. You may hear a mental health diagnosis and think that your coparent can't possibly be a good parent. This is not so. Your coparent may need support to stabilize but can be a good parent with a mental health diagnosis. It depends on the particular diagnosis and how your ex responds to medication and treatment.

Many people with mental illness live full and productive lives. You would never know to meet them that they even have a mental illness. A person with a mood disorder such as depression or panic disorder can take medication and be an excellent parent.

The problem is that stress tends to make any mental illness

worse. The stress of divorce can trigger a need for an adjustment in medication dosages or for more intensive therapy. The Parenting Coordinator will work with the parent's therapist and psychiatrist as part of the team to be sure that mental health issues are addressed. This may simply mean verifying that medications are being taken regularly or determining the impact of the mental health issues on parenting. For example, a person with a paranoid disorder may be bright and competent in most areas of functioning, but may look at the world with mistrust and suspicion. The question then becomes whether her "paranoia" has a negative impact on her ability to parent. Does her paranoid impair her ability to make good judgments about her children or is she able to function adequately as a parent? The Parenting Coordinator can help get this question answered.

The key to managing bumps in the road with mental illness is to watch for those bumps. You may notice odd behavior: mood swings or depression, for example. The children may say, "Dad is sleeping all the time. He hardly eats anything, just cooks for us and goes back to bed. He just doesn't seem to care much anymore. Is he all right?" You may need to ask your coparent if he has stopped taking his medication. You may also need to suggest that your coparent seek professional help. Your Parenting Coordinator will be able to provide referrals for your coparent or he can check with your local community mental health center. Whatever you do, don't ignore it. Mental illness is very treatable, but needs to be treated quickly for the best results.

Addiction

Addiction can take many forms. People can be addicted to alcohol, smoking, drugs, gambling, food, or sex. Some people have addictive personalities; these people can become addicted easily. Some people never overcome addictions, while others can recover and be good parents.

The parenting plan will need to address addiction, for the safety of the children. A parent who still uses drugs may need drug testing prior to any parenting time or may need to use a supervised visitation center to see the children. A recently recovered alcoholic may need a referral to both counseling and Alcoholics Anonymous. The coparent may wish to attend Al-Anon or another such support group.

You should know the signs of addiction, not only to recognize a problem with your ex, but also to be alert for problems that may crop up in yourself. Divorce is a stressful time. It is easy to self-medicate with alcohol or prescription drugs, or to feel better by gambling or having sex with multiple partners. Knowing the signs of addiction can help you to reach out for help before it is too late.

Here are some signs of addiction:

- Mood changes or mood swings—happy one moment and depressed the next
- Unexplained (and unintended) weight loss
- Pupils of the eye are larger or smaller than usual
- Sleep schedule is very different than usual—sleeping more, less, or at different times; hard to wake up from sleep
- Runny nose without any other signs of a cold or allergy
- Having more money than usual and then having little or none
- Lying, sneaking out of the house, hanging up the phone quickly when you come near
- Stealing
- Suddenly and urgently needing to leave the house
- Drug paraphernalia—scales, papers, needles, etc.

Be alert for these signs, not only in you and your coparent, but also in your children. Addiction among teenagers is a very real problem. Studies have shown that children whose parents divorce when the children are teenagers are more likely to be involved with drugs.

The problem with addiction is that it is much easier to see it in someone else than in yourself. This is because one of the primary symptoms of addiction is *denial*. Denial is the voice in your head that says, "I don't have a problem. I can stop anytime." This is your first warning bell. Can you really stop anytime? And not start again? Think about that for a while.

Denial comes in many different ways. Some are things the addict says to himself, some are things others say.

I have to drink (take drugs, gamble, etc.) every day for it to be a problem.

Not true. It's a problem if it causes problems. Are you late to pick up the children? Forgot to attend the parent-teacher meeting? Slept through the school play? Chronically late to work after the weekend? If these were caused by the addictive behavior, there is a problem.

My ex drove me to take drugs.

Blaming others is the easy way out. *Not my fault; she made me do it.* But it's simply not true. Every person is in charge of his own behavior.

If I pay off my ex's gambling debts, he won't gamble again.

This is called enabling behavior. It enables, or helps, the person continue in the addictive behavior.

Drinking isn't a problem if I can keep my job.

The problem is not just keeping a job. The problem is all the things needed to be a good parent: problem-solving, being on time, being present, and bringing your whole self to your role as a parent.

If you or your children are referred for counseling or a family support group such as Al-Anon, take a deep breath and go. There is scientific evidence that children who attended counseling showed reduced marijuana, alcohol, and other illegal drug use and number of sexual partners during the teen years compared to teens who did not attend counseling. Other studies show that teenagers whose mothers attended counseling, even if the teenagers did not go themselves, had fewer symptoms of mental health problems and were less likely to use or abuse alcohol, marijuana, and other illegal drug use.

Violence

Violence in the home or by family members is called domestic violence or intimate partner violence. The National Coalition Against Domestic Violence (NCADV) defines it this way:

- Actual or threatened physical harm
- Sexual assault
- Name-calling or put downs.
- Keeping a partner from calling their family or friends
- Stopping a partner from getting or keeping a job
- Withholding money
- Stalking
- Intimidation
- Chronic situations in which one person controls or intends to control another person's behavior

- Misuse of power that may result in injury or harm to the psychological, social, economic, sexual, or physical well-being of family members

Some violence between couples is one-sided. One person hits, the other person is hurt. The hitter is usually the man, almost 90 percent of the time, but can be the woman. A person who is violent to someone in a family relationship is called a "batterer." The person who is injured is "battered." These terms paint a picture of what is happening. This kind of violence is raw and angry. The batterer is often looking for control over the other person. Violence and intimidation are the ways he will try to gain that control.

Batterers tend to be very jealous and possessive. *The other person is "mine."* Batterers will do things like sell one car so that it's hard for their partner to get around, even to work. They will dole out small amounts of money so the other person can't buy a bus ticket out of town. Batterers will limit contact with family and friends, "I don't want you seeing that friend Rachel anymore. Don't answer the phone when she calls."

Some people grew up surrounded by violence. They may not be aware of what society regards as normal, expected behavior and what is out of bounds. Here are some specific actions that are considered domestic violence:

Psychological Abuse
- Cursing, demeaning, yelling, taunting
- Isolating, coercing, threatening harm
- Stalking, harassing, making a person afraid

Physical Abuse
- Slapping, grabbing, shoving, twisting arm, pulling hair
- Kicking, punching, biting, throwing things

- Choking, using guns and knives, mutilating, burning

Sexual Abuse

- Raping, forcing unwanted sexual behaviors, coercing, harassing

Financial Abuse

- Controlling purchases, holding back money and information

Notice all the different ways domestic violence happens. It is not just physical violence. Emotional violence can be just as violent, and just as damaging. Also, physical violence does not have to happen over and over again. A one-time event can give the batterer the control he wants.

Remember Thanksgiving

Jessica and John (not their real names) had been married for six months when Thanksgiving rolled around. John asked Jessica to prepare a traditional turkey dinner with stuffing, pumpkin pies, and red wine. Jessica went to the store but forgot to buy the wine. On the morning of Thanksgiving, John flew into a rage when he found Jessica had not bought the wine. He punched Jessica, threw the food on the floor, and smashed china plates and wine glasses. Then he called his family and told them Jessica was ill and the Thanksgiving feast was canceled. John never beat Jessica after that. If she did not do as he told her, he simply said, "Remember Thanksgiving."

Some violence between couples happens only in a certain situation. The couple is arguing, and one will shove the other. Neither person is injured. They are not afraid of each other after this incident. In more than half of these cases, both people acted in a violent way. The behavior comes from not having good skills in dealing with conflict. Either, or both, people may simply not know how to manage what is going on. Shoving the other person is a kind of communication. Not a good kind, but it is communication. *I am so frustrated and angry, I have no idea what to say or do next.* This kind of violence usually stops after separation, but not always.

Separation, however, is the most dangerous time for the person who has been battered. The batterer, who is looking for control, is now not in control. The danger is even more if the batterer has destroyed property in the past, injured pets, or threatened to kidnap or harm his children. Other events can also add to the feeling of loss of control, such as being laid off or facing a reduction in hours at work.

Statistics show that most victims of domestic violence try to leave the batterer six times before they are actually able to get away (Fleming, et al, 2012). The emotional abuse from the batterer has left the victim feeling unworthy and unable to plan.

IF YOU NEED HELP

If you or someone you know is a victim of domestic violence, reach out for help now. If you are working with a Parenting Coordinator, ask for help. Also, call the National Domestic Violence Hotline at 1-800-799-SAFE (7233) or the National Sexual Assault Hotline at 1-800-656-4673.

Remember, computer use can be tracked. A batterer can check the history of websites visited—and most likely *will* check. If you are afraid your Internet and/or computer usage might be monitored, please use a safer computer (at a location the batterer cannot access), or call the National Domestic Violence Hotline.

Protection for All

Some states and provinces will not allow parenting coordination if there is a history of domestic violence in a marriage. Some will allow it if the violence did not happen often and is not currently happening. Courts will be careful to make sure children are safe. The parenting plan may include supervised visits. Or the plan may call for handing off the children someplace other than home—a neutral, safe site. It is important to inform the Parenting Coordinator about any violence in the marriage—emotional, sexual, or physical. You and the children may not be safe otherwise.

Emotions run high in a difficult divorce. When you and your ex are filled with anger, either of you may act in ways that you usually would not. Your "filter" of behavior that normally keeps you calm and reasonable does not work as well. You may be more impulsive. You may say or do things that you regret later. But in the heat of the moment, you do not think ahead about the effect your words or actions will have on your ex or your children. You or your ex may be on your worst behavior rather than your best behavior.

A judge once commented, "In criminal court, we see bad people at their best. Criminals are dressed in suits, looking like model citizens. But in divorce court, we see good people at their worst. Normally well-behaved people say and do things they would never imagine they were capable of. It's sad, but true."

Because of the high emotions and tendency toward poor behavior among divorcing couples, many Parenting Coordinators do not allow large bags or briefcases to be brought into sessions. Weapons are specifically forbidden. It may seem odd to have to remind an adult not to bring a weapon to a professional appointment. But a high-conflict divorce can bring with it high-conflict behavior. Do not be offended if the Parenting Coordinator brings up the subject of weapons. It is for everyone's protection.

In very high-conflict divorces, the Parenting Coordinator may have the parents come into the office via different entrances. Sometimes one parent is asked to leave first, and the second parent leaves after the other has driven away, as an extra safety measure. This gives a safety cushion of space until emotions are more under control.

Do not make a direct threat to your ex or the Parenting Coordinator during a parenting coordination session. The Parenting Coordinator may report the threat to law enforcement. "I didn't mean it" will not take back the intent. The threat was meant at the moment it was said. Some people use words as weapons. Take time to cool down if you feel the urge to make a threat. "Give me a minute, please" is an acceptable way to let the angry moment pass.

Watch for Falling Rocks

As you drive through the mountains you notice signs that read, "Watch for falling rocks." Parenting after a divorce is a lot like this. The road twists and turns. You have to stay alert because a rock may loosen itself and fall toward your moving car. The sign reminds you to look ahead to see what rocks might be falling. Likewise, knowing what potential "rocks" may obstruct your path as you begin coparenting after divorce helps you avoid them and keep yourself and your children safe.

CHAPTER 8

Are We There Yet?

When Does It End?

When the parenting coordination process works well, it is easy to tell when parenting coordination should end. Parents are no longer locked in conflict. Or they can manage their differences so the children are not exposed to their conflict. Decisions about the children are made for the children's benefit. The children are not used as weapons of revenge or pawns to "win" the game of divorce.

This doesn't mean that parenting is now magically easy. Successful parenting is one of the hardest jobs on earth. It is never easy, just less difficult. The success of parenting is seen in well-adjusted children. Not perfect children, since that is unrealistic for any parent to expect. But children who know their place in the world, and know they are loved—by both of their parents.

Even though there may be bumps in the road ahead, you have the tools you need to move forward without the help of a Parenting Coordinator. You have learned the "dance" of coparenting. The steps have changed from the dance you knew before the divorce. But now you know the new steps and can move without stepping on anyone's toes.

The cycle of parenting coordination starts with frequent sessions while parenting goals are set and issues are identified. Then sessions are spaced farther apart as the parenting plan settles into a routine. The parenting plan is reviewed for needed changes at certain trigger points:

- Change from elementary to middle school
- Change from middle school to high school
- Remarriage
- Change in living arrangements (or one both parents moving)
- Any other change that affects the children's well-being

You have learned that a decision made for a child when she is five years old is probably not the best decision for her when she is thirteen. You and your ex have learned how to make changes without making war. The Florida law regarding divorce sums it up well: coparents "share the rights, responsibilities, and joys of parenting."

This does not mean that you cannot go back to the Parenting Coordinator for a checkup or tune-up. Some of my clients call after a year or two, needing a specific problem addressed. A checkup may find that the parents have fallen back into bad habits of communication. Or the children have entered a new developmental phase that the parents were not aware of. This does not mean the parents are "bad parents." A quick tune-up can get better communication and problem-solving strategies in place. Then the parents are on their way again.

Calling It Quits

Sometimes, though, parenting coordination sessions are stopped because they are no longer effective or appropriate. One or both parents can lose trust in the Parenting Coordinator due to a breach of ethics. While an ethics problem is rare, it can happen. You may remember the case mentioned earlier of the parent who traded meals at the restaurant he owned for the cost of parenting coordination sessions. Even if the Parenting Coordinator vowed to remain completely impartial, there would still be the possibility that the Parenting Coordinator would treat him a little differently.

Ethical guidelines for Parenting Coordinators state that there should not be even the *appearance* of impropriety. In the restaurant example, it looked as if the Parenting Coordinator might give special treatment to the parent who owned the restaurant. Even if this didn't actually happen, the Parenting Coordinator should not have allowed a situation to develop where it looks as if it might happen.

Dual roles are also conflicts of interest. A Parenting Coordinator should not also be the family lawyer, therapist, or mediator—that is a *dual role*. Having just one role prevents the appearance of favoritism to either parent.

An important part of the professional relationship with the Parenting Coordinator is that it is . . . professional. The Parenting Coordinator is not a friend or buddy. Friendly, yes, but not a friend. For parents with boundary issues this can be a problem. Some parents are lonely during the divorce process and look for a friend. The Parenting Coordinator will be supportive. The Parenting Coordinator will help find solutions. But the Parenting Coordinator will only be a professional resource, not a friend.

The Parenting Coordinator will step down if it is no longer possible to be impartial. The Parenting Coordinator will not accept favors or loans from either parent. A favor or a loan would make it hard for the Parenting Coordinator to remain neutral. However, in this case neutral is a misleading word, because the

Parenting Coordinator is in favor of the best decision for the children. If there is any partiality in a Parenting Coordinator, it will be toward the children. This is, after all, the focus of the Parenting Coordinator: the well-being of the children.

The Parenting Coordinator is a professional. Parents need to respect the rules set up for parenting coordination sessions just as they would respect a visit to a doctor or a lawyer. Negative feelings about the coparent should not affect the rules of behavior. Keeping appointments, completing tasks as assigned, and being courteous are all expected as part of the process.

Safety is a reason that a Parenting Coordinator will step down. An actively violent parent will cause the Parenting Coordinator to notify the court and stop sessions. Watching out for safety concerns is an ongoing process for the Parenting Coordinator. Some parents become violent if they don't think they are getting their way in the parenting coordination process. For safety's sake, violence cannot be tolerated.

Anger can be shown in violence but can also be shown in other ways. Some parents make false claims of abuse as an attack on their ex. The Parenting Coordinator is required to report any claim of abuse or neglect to the state and provincial authorities. But the Parenting Coordinator may keep working with the parents if it looks as if the parent made the abuse claim just to harass the other parent.

Threatening a lawsuit is another way a parent may show anger. "I'll sue you if you _____". Fill in the blank with some version of "don't do what I want." Angry parents may have been in the court system so long that this seems like a good way to get the Parenting Coordinator to do what they want. However, a civil case against a Parenting Coordinator must prove "harm." This is difficult to do, especially when the only harm is to the parent's need for control.

Most parenting coordination requires the parents to meet with the Parenting Coordinator to resolve issues when there is a complaint. This can allow the Parenting Coordinator to point out the underlying issue to the angry parent so the real work of parenting coordination can continue.

Parenting coordination will also end if the legal jurisdiction changes. All cases close when the youngest child in the family reaches the age of "majority," usually eighteen years old.

Boundaries

Boundaries are lines of behavior that should not be crossed. We talked about some of these earlier. Angry parents can intentionally violate boundaries as a way to derail the parenting coordination process. The angry parent reasons that, if there are enough roadblocks thrown up, the parenting coordination process will stop. Either the other parent or the Parenting Coordinator will just give up.

Just as you can predict how your child might misbehave, the Parenting Coordinator knows that some of this behavior is going to happen. "Forgetting" what was agreed upon, not paying fees, not being flexible in scheduling appointments, trying to give the Parenting Coordinator gifts ... the Parenting Coordinator has seen it all. Like a good parent, the Parenting Coordinator sets boundaries and keeps them. By the way, boundaries include behavior with the office staff as well as the Parenting Coordinator.

There is a flip side to the controlling parent. A parent may, instead of showing bad behavior, push the opposite boundary.

The "Nice Guy" approach is one where the parent heaps the Parenting Coordinator with compliments. The Nice Guy declares that there is no better Parenting Coordinator in the universe. These parents are not so discreetly trying to win the Parenting Coordinator over to "their" side. It is just as much a boundary problem as angry, complaining behavior.

Another variation of the Nice Guy is the rich or famous parent. This parent (or parents; two can play this game) tries to influence the Parenting Coordinator by her status. These parents make sure to mention famous friends, their many homes or cars, and their rich lifestyle. While it may not be entirely calculated, the basic intent is to get the Parenting Coordinator to think their way. Some well-respected professionals who come to parenting coordination sessions may do the same thing. The firefighter, religious leader, or charity administrator may try to trade "goodwill points" during sessions, thinking this will influence the Parenting Coordinator to his way of thinking.

Your own boundaries are important to recognize. As a parent, you have your own limits, both physical and emotional. There is an acronym in twelve-step programs that is useful here. HALT is a reminder that you should never allow yourself to be too *hungry, angry, lonely,* or *tired.* This means that you don't come to parenting coordination sessions after three hours of sleep. It also means that you don't call your ex to work out a problem with the children if you are already angry. HALT. Take care of the hunger, anger, loneliness, or tiredness first.

As a reminder, here are some boundaries for parenting coordination sessions:

- No yelling at the other parent, the Parenting Coordinator, or office staff.

- No interrupting or speaking over the other person. Everyone gets a turn.
- No distractions. Turn off the cell phone. Stay focused.
- No "kitchen sinking"—deal only with the issue at hand. Don't bring up anything (or everything) else.

And, here's the primary reminder:

Focus on the best interests of your children.

Parenting coordination can be a valuable resource for you and your children. As you move through the process, allow the Parenting Coordinator to guide you, your coparent, and the other members of your parenting team (relatives, teachers, doctors, and others) toward the best plan for allowing your children to grow into healthy adults. It is a journey of change, and one well worth taking.

CHAPTER 9

Resources

Useful Websites and Books for Parents and Children
The Internet offers many free resources that can help in creating and maintaining your parenting plan. The list here is but a sampling of the websites available. Follow the links at the websites listed for even more resources. Your Parenting Coordinator may have additional resources for you that are specific to your area or your particular needs.

The book list is also not exhaustive, but has a good mix of reading for parents and children. Many of the books may be helpful to others on the parenting team—grandparents, aunts and uncles, and other caregivers.

Websites

Long-Distance Contact and Virtual Visitation
Virtual Visitation — http://www.internetvisitation.org
Distance Parent — http://www.distanceparent.org
Separated Parenting Access and Resource Center—
http://www.deltabravo.net
Parenting from a Distance: A how-to guide published by the University of Nebraska —
http://www.ianrpubs.unl.edu/sendIt/g1996.pdf
Our Family Wizard: subscription to shared family calendars, journals, and other resources —
http://www.ourfamilywizard.com/index.cfm

Divorce Info: Loving Your Kids Across the Miles —
http://www.divorceinfo.com/kidsacrossmiles.htm

Family Focused Digital Calendar
http://www.ourfamilywizard.com
http://www.calendarwiz.com/index.php
https://www.google.com/calendar
http://www.kincafe.com

General Parenting Information
http://www.afccnet.org/resource-center/resources-for-families/
categoryid/1
http://www.uptoparents.org
http://www.helpguide.org/articles/family-divorce/co-
parenting-tips-for-divorced-parents.htm
http://www.childcentereddivorce.com/
http://www.divorcesupport.com
http://www.healthyparent.com

Kids Sites
http://kids.aol.com/KOL/

Websites to Search for Kids Software
http://kids.getnetwise.org/

CoParenting Class
https://www.onlineparentingprograms.com/online-classes/
high-conflict-and-anger-class.html

CoParent Communication Site
https://www.propercomm.com/

Direct Communication over the Internet
www.skype.com
www.apple.com/ios/facetime

Web-Based Scrapbooks and Photo/Video Sharing Services
www.dropshots.com/
www.flickr.com
www.smugmug.com
www.webshots.com
www.photobucket.com
www.fotki.com
www.famzam.com
www.phanfare.com
www.joomeo.com
www.picasa.google.com

Websites That Offer Parental Internet Controls
Windows
http://windows.microsoft.com/en-us/windows/security-privacy-accounts-help#security-privacy-accounts-help=windows-7&v0h=win8tab1&v1h=win8tab1&v2h=win7tab3&v3h=winvistatab1
America Online — https://parentalcontrols.aol.com
Apple
http://theappleblog.com/2009/01/13/kid-proofing-a-mac-with-parental-controls/

Links to Software and Information—Parental Controls on the Internet
Kaspersky Internet Security 7.0
http://kaspersky.com

Safe Eyes
www.internetsafety.com—replaced http://safeeyes.com
Guardian Monitor Professional
http://www.guardiansoft.com
CyberPatrol
http://www.cyberpatrol.com
Computer Cop
http://www.computercop.com

Links to Contact Guidelines or Sample Plans with a Long-Distance or Travel Component
Some of these links are to handbooks or articles that may take a while to download. Wait while the material loads on your computer.
Arizona Supreme Court Model, Planning for Parenting Time
http://azcourts.gov/Portals/31/ParentingTime/
PPWguidelines.pdf
Lucas County, Ohio, Distance Parenting Schedule
http://co.lucas.oh.us/documents/79/
LongDistanceCourtSchedule.PDF
Tuscarawas County, Long-Distance Parenting Orders and
Incidental Rules
http://www.co.tuscarawas.oh.us/Common%20Pleas/Legal%20
Information/LongDistanceOrder.pdf
New Hampshire Check-Off Parenting Plan
http://www.courts.state.nh.us/forms/nhjb-2064-fs.pdf
New York Check-Off Parenting Plan
http://www.courts.state.ny.us/forms/matrimonial/Parenting-
Plan-Form.pdf
Oklahoma Standard Visitation Schedule with Forms http://
www.oscn.net/forms/aoc_form/adobe/Form.76.pdf

Reading List: Divorce

Books for Parents

Beyer, R. & Winchester, K. (2001). *Juggling Act: Handling Divorce without Dropping the Ball: A Survival Kit for Parents and Kids*. Free Spirit Publishing.

Daughtry, T. (2011). *Co-Parenting Works!: Helping Your Children Thrive after Divorce*. Zondervan.

Emery, R. (2006). *The Truth about Children and Divorce: Dealing with the Emotions So You and Your Children Can Thrive*. Plume.

Ford-Blackstone, J. & Jupe, S. (2004). *Ex-Etiquette for Parents: Good Behavior after a Divorce or Separation*. Chicago Review Press.

Gaies, J. S., & Morris, J. M., Jr. (2014). *Mindful Co-parenting: A Child-Friendly Path through Divorce*. CreateSpace Independent Publishing.

Garber, B. (2008). *Keeping Kids Out of the Middle: Child-Centered Parenting in the Midst of Conflict, Separation, and Divorce*. Health Communications, Inc.

Hannibal, M. E. (2006). *Good Parenting Through Your Divorce: The Essential Guidebook to Helping Your Children Adjust and Thrive*. Da Capo Press.

Hetherington, E. M. & Kelly, J. (2003). *For Better or For Worse: Divorce Reconsidered*. W. W. Norton & Company.

Jones-Soderman, J., Quattrocchi, A. & Steinberg, S. (2006). *How to Talk to Your Children about Divorce*. Family Mediation Center Publishing Company.

Lieberman, A. (1995). *The Emotional Life of the Toddler*. Free Press.

Lippman, J. & Greenwall Lewis, P. (2008) *Divorcing with Children: Expert Answers to Tough Questions from Parents and Children.* Praeger.

Long, N. & Forehand, R. (2002). *Making Divorce Easier on Your Child: 50 Effective Ways to Help Children Adjust.* McGraw-Hill.

McGhee, C. (2010). *Parenting Apart: How Separated and Divorced Parents Can Raise Happy and Secure Kids.* Berkley Trade.

McHale, J. (2007). *Charting the Bumpy Road of Coparenthood: Understanding the Challenges of Family Life.* Zero to Three.

Moran, J., Sullivan, T. & Sullivan, M. (2014). Overcoming the Co-Parenting Trap: Essential Parenting Skills When a Child Resists a Parent, Overcoming Barriers, Inc.

Neuman, G. & Romanowski, P. (1999). *Helping Your Kids Cope with Divorce the Sandcastles Way.* Random House.

Pedro-Carroll, J. (2010). *Putting Children First: Proven Parenting Strategies for Helping Children Thrive Through Divorce.* Avery Trade.

Philyaw, D. & Thomas, M. (2013). *Co-Parenting 101: Helping Your Kids Thrive in Two Households after Divorce.* New Harbinger Publications.

Rios, S. (2009). *The 7 Fatal Mistakes Divorced and Separated Parents Make: Strategies for Raising Healthy Children of Divorce and Conflict.* Life Threads Books.

Ross, J. & Corcoran, J. (2011). *Joint Custody with a Jerk: Raising a Child with an Uncooperative Ex.* St. Martin's Griffin.

Schneider, M. & Zuckerberg, J. (1996). *Difficult Questions Kids Ask and Are Afraid to Ask about Divorce.* Touchstone.

Thayer, E. & Zimmerman, J. (2001). *The Co-Parenting Survival Guide: Letting Go of Conflict after a Difficult Divorce.* New Harbinger Publications.

Thomas, S. (2004). *Parents Are Forever: A Step-by-Step Guide to Becoming Successful Coparents after Divorce.* Springboard Publications.

Wallerstein, J. (2004). *What about the Kids?: Raising Your Children Before, During, and After Divorce.* Hyperion.

Warshak, R. (2010). *Divorce Poison: How to Protect Your Family From Bad-Mouthing and Brainwashing.* William Morrow Paperbacks.

Wolf, A. E. (1998). *Why Did You Have to Get a Divorce? And Why Can't I Get a Hamster? A Guide to Parenting through Divorce.* Farrar Straus & Giroux.

Books for Children

Bauer, R. (2015). *Percy's Imperfectly Perfect Family*, Archway Publishing.

Brown, M. & Brown, L. K. (1988). *Dinosaurs Divorce: A Guide for Changing Families.* Little, Brown Books for Young Readers.

Cassella-Kapusinski, L. (2006). *Now What Do I Do?: A Guide to Help Teenagers with Their Parents' Separation or Divorce.* ACTA Publications.

Ford, M. (2006). *My Parents Are Divorced Too: A Book for Kids by Kids.* Magination Press.

Foster, B. L. (2006). *The Way They Were: Dealing with Your Parents' Divorce After a Lifetime of Marriage.* Three Rivers Press.

Holyoke, N. (2009). *A Smart Girl's Guide to Her Parents' Divorce: How to Land on Your Feet When Your World Turns Upside Down.* American Girl.

LaMotte, E. (2008). *Overcoming Your Parents' Divorce: 5 Steps to a Happy Relationship.* New Horizons Press.

Lansky, V. (1997). *It's Not Your Fault, Koko Bear: A Read-Together Book for Parents and Young Children during Divorce.* Book Peddlers.

Levins, S. (2006). *Was It the Chocolate Pudding?: A Story for Little Kids about Divorce.* American Psychology Association.

Masurel, C. (2003). *Two Homes.* Candlewick.

MacGregor, C. (2001). *The Divorce Help Book for Kids.* Impact Publishers.

———. (2004). *The Divorce Help Book for Teens.* Impact Publishers.

Moore-Mallinos, J. (2005). *When My Parents Forgot How to be Friends (Let's Talk About It!).* Barron's Educational Series.

Sindell, M. (2007). *The Bright Side: Surviving Your Parents' Divorce.* HCI Press.

Smith, S. Smith, L. & Smith, A. (2012). *Divorce Survival Guide for Kids: Tips to Survive Your Parents' Divorce: For Kids, Written by Kids.* Create Space Independent Publishing Platform.

Stern, Z. & Stern, E. (2008) *Divorce Is Not the End of the World: Zoe's and Evan's Coping Guide for Kids.* Tricycle Press.

Reading List: Blending Families

Books for Parents

Buscemi, K. (2011). *I Do, Part 2: How to Survive Divorce, Co-Parent Your Kids, and Blend Your Families without Losing Your Mind.* NorLightsPress.

Cress Dudley, S. (2009). *Blended Family Advice: A Step-by-Step Guide to Help Blended and Step Families Become Strong and Successful.* Xlibris.

Deal, R. (2006). *The Smart Stepfamily: Seven Steps to a Healthy Family.* Bethany House Publishing.

———. (2011). *The Smart Stepdad: Steps to Help You Succeed.* Bethany House Publishing.

Deal, R. & Petherbridge, L. (2009). *The Smart Stepmom: Practical Steps to Help You Thrive.* Bethany House Publishing.

Ford, J. & Chase, A. (2009). *Wonderful Ways to Be a Stepparent.* Red Wheel/Weiser.

Frisbie, D. & Frisbie, L. (2005). *Happily Remarried: Making Decisions Together, Blending Families Successfully, Building a Love That Will Last.* Harvest House Publishers.

Katz, R. (2010). *The Happy Stepmother: Stay Sane, Empower Yourself, Thrive in Your New Family.* Harlequin.

Lintermans, G. (2011). *The Secrets of Stepfamily Success.* Llumina Press.

Marsolini, M. (2006). *Raising Children in Blended Families: Helpful Insights, Expert Opinions, and True Stories.* Kregel Publications.

Martin, W. (2009). *Stepmonster: A New Look at Why Real Stepmothers Think, Feel, and Act the Way We Do.* Houghton Mifflin Harcourt.

Munroe, E. & Levine, I. (2009). *The Everything Guide to Stepparenting: Practical, Reassuring Advice for Creating Healthy, Long-Lasting Relationships.* Adams Media.

Pedro-Carroll, J. (2010). *Putting Children First: Proven Parenting Strategies for Helping Children Thrive Through Divorce.* Avery Trade.

Penton, J. and Welsh, S. (2007). *Yours, Mine, and Hours: Relationship Skills for Blended Families.* BookSurge Publishing.

Pickhardt, C. (2010). *Keys to Successful Stepfathering.* Barron's Educational Series.

Weiss-Wisdom, D. (2012). *Wisdom on Step-Parenting: How to Succeed Where Others Fail.* Create Space Independent Publishing Platform.

Wenck, S. & Hansen, C. (2009). *Love Him, Love His Kids: The Stepmother's Guide to Surviving and Thriving in a Blended Family.* Adams Media.

Wisdom, S. & Green, J. (2002). *Stepcoupling: Creating and Sustaining a Strong Marriage in Today's Blended Family.* Three Rivers Press.

Books for Children/Teens

Block, J., Bartell, S. & Frantz, J. (2001). *Stepliving for Teens: Getting Along with Stepparents, Parents, and Siblings.* Price, Stern, Sloan.

Butcher, T. (2011). *My Bonus Mom: Taking the Step Out of Stepmom.* Little Five Star.

Chambers, P. (2008). *My Mommy's Getting Married.* Infinity Publishing Company.

Cohn, L. & Glasser, D. (2008) *The Step-Tween Survival Guide: How to Deal with Life in a Stepfamily.* Free Spirit Publishing.

Crist, J. & Verdick, E. (2010). *Siblings: You're Stuck with Each Other, So Stick Together.* Free Spirit Publishing.

Hugo, L. (2005). *Jessica's Two Families: Helping Children Learn to Cope with Blended Households.* New Horizon Press.

Lewis, S. (2009). *Do You Sing Twinkle?: A Story about Remarriage and New Family.* Magination Press.

Lipscomb Deppe, W. (2010). *Diary of a Stepkid: A Guided Journal for Tweens and Teens.* Create Space Independent Platform.

McCann, M. (2001). *Chelsea's Tree: A story for Step Children and Stepkids.* Inspiration Publications.

Reading List: General Parenting

Books for Parents

Faber, A. & Mazlish, E. (2012). *How to Talk So Kids Will Listen & Listen So Kids Will Talk.* Scribner Press.

Feiler, B. (2013). *The Secrets of Happy Families: Improve Your Mornings, Rethink Family Dinner, Fight Smarter, Go Out and Play, and Much More.* William Morrow.

Hemmen, L. (2012). *Parenting a Teen Girl: A Crash Course on Conflict, Communication and Connection with Your Teenage Daughter.* New Harbinger Publications.

James, S. & Thomas, D. (2009). *Wild Things: The Art of Nurturing Boys.* Tyndale House Publishers, Inc.

Kenney, L. & Young, W. (2015). *Bloom: 50 Things to Say, Think, and Do With Angry, Anxious, and Over-the-Top Kids.* Unhooked Books.

Markham, L. (2012). *Peaceful Parent, Happy Kids: How to Stop Yelling and Start Connecting.* Perigee Trade.

Nelsen, J. (2006). *Positive Discipline.* Ballantine Books.

Runkel, H. (2008). *Screamfree Parenting: The Revolutionary Approach to Raising Your Kids by Keeping Your Cool.* Three Rivers Press.

Sells, S. (2002). *Parenting Your Out-of-Control Teenager: 7 Steps to Reestablish Authority and Reclaim Love.* St. Martin's Griffin.

Siegel, D. & Hartzell, M. (2004). *Parenting from the Inside Out.* Tarcher.

Stiffelman, S. (2012.) *Parenting without Power Struggles: Raising Joyful, Resilient Kids While Staying Cool, Calm, and Connected.* Atria Book.

Books for Children

Cook, J. (2011). *I Just Don't Like the Sound of No! My Story about Accepting No for an Answer and Disagreeing the Right Way!* Boys Town Press.

———. (2012). *Teamwork Isn't My Thing, and I Don't Like to Share!* Boys Town Press.

———. (2012). *Sorry, I Forgot to Ask!: My Story about Asking Permission and Making and Apology.* Boys Town Press.

Crist, J. (2004). *What to Do When You're Scared and Worried: A Guide for Kids.* Free Spirit Publishing.

Javernick, E. (2010). *What If Everybody Did That?* Two Lions.

Moser, A. (1996). *Don't Pop Your Cork on Mondays!* Landmark Editions.

———. (1996). *Don't Feed the Monster on Tuesdays!* Landmark Editions.

———. (1996). *Don't Rant and Rave on Wednesdays!* Landmark Editions.

————. (1996) *Don't Despair on Thursdays!* Landmark Editions.

————. (1999) *Don't Tell a Whopper on Fridays!: The Children's Truth Control Book*, Landmark Editions.

————. (2000). *Don't Fall Apart on Saturdays!: The Children's Divorce-Survival Book.* Landmark Editions.

————. (1996). *Don't Be a Menace on Sundays!: The Children's Anti-Violence Book.* Landmark Editions.

Sornson, B. (2013). *Stand in My Shoes: Kids Learning About Empathy.* Love and Logic Press.

References

Amato, P. R. (2010). Research on divorce: Continuing trends and new developments. *Journal of Marriage and Family,* 72(3), 650–666.

Brody, G.H. & Neubaum, E. (1996). Family transitions as stressors in children and adolescents. In C.R. Pfeffer (Ed.), *Severe Stress and Mental Disturbance in Children.* Washington, D.C.: American Psychiatric Press, 559-590.

Carter, D.K. (2011). *Parenting Coordination: A Practical Guide for Family Law Professionals.* Springer Publishing.

Cashmore, J., Parkinson, P., Taylor, A. (2008). Overnight Stays and Children's Relationships With Resident and Nonresident Parents After Divorce, *Journal of Family Issues,* 29 (6), 707-733.

Divorce Fact Sheet (2012), Stats Canada, http://www.separation.ca/pdfs/divorcefacts.pdf.

Emery, R.E., & Coiro, M.J. (1995). Divorce: Consequences for children. *Pediatric Review,* 16, 306–10.

Fabricius, W.V., Sokol, K.R., Diaz, P., & Braver, S.L. (2014).

Parenting time, parent conflict, parent-child relationships, and children's physical health. In K. Kuehnle, & L. Drozd (Eds.), *Parenting Plan Evaluations: Applied Research for the Family Court.* Oxford University Press, 188-213.

Fieldstone, L., Lee, M. C., Baker, J. K., & McHale, J. P. (2012). Perspectives on parenting coordination: Views of Parenting Coordinators, attorneys, and judiciary members. *Family Court Review*, 50(3), 441–454.

Fleming, K., Newton, T., Fernandez-Botran, Mille, J, & Ellison Burn, V. (2012). *Intimate Partner Stalking Victimization and Posttraumatic Stress Symptoms in Post-Abuse Women,* Violence Against Women, 18(12), 1368-1389.

Furstenberg, F. F. Jr, & Cherlin, A. J. (1991). *Divided Families: What Happens to Children When Parents Part.* Harvard University Press.

Gottman, J. M. & Silver, N. (1999). *The Seven Principles for Making Marriages Work,* New York: Three Rivers Press.

Grych, J.H. & Fincham, F.D. (1992). Interventions for children of divorce: Toward greater integration of research and action. *Psychological Bulletin*, 111, 434-454.

Hartnup T. (1996). Divorce and marital strife and their effects on children. *Arch Dis Child*, 75, 1–8.

Hayes, S., Grady, M., & Brantley, H. (2012). E-mails, statutes, and personality disorders: A contextual examination of the processes, interventions, and perspective of Parenting Coordinators. *Family Court Review*, 50(3), 429–440.

Henry, W., Fieldstone, L., & Bohac, K. (2009). Parenting coordination and court relitigation: A case study. *Family Court Review*, 47(4), 682–697.

Hetherington, E. M., & Stanley-Hagan, M. (1999). The adjustment of children with divorced parents: a risk and resiliency perspective. *J Child Psychol Psychiatry*, 40, 129–40.

Jaffe, P. G., Johnston, J. R., Crooks, C. V., and Bala, N. (2008), Custody disputes involving allegations of domestic violence: Toward a differentiated approach to parenting plans. *Family Court Review*, 46, 500–522.

Kelly, J., & Emery, R. E. (2003). Children's adjustment following divorce: Risk and resilience perspectives. *Family Relations*, 52, 352–362

Kelly, J. B. (1998). Marital conflict, divorce, and children's adjustment. *Child Adolesc Psychiatr Clin N Am*, 7, 259–271.

Kids Count Data Center (2015). The Annie E. Casey Foundation, www.datacenter.kidscount.org

Lamb, M. E. (Ed.). (2010). *The Role of the Father in Child Development* (fifth edition). Wiley.

McIntosh, J. E., Pruett, M. K., & Kelly, J. B. (2014). Parental separation and overnight care of young children, part ii: Putting theory into practice. *Family Court Review*, 52, 256–262.

National Coalition Against Domestic Violence, www.ncadv. org.

Needle, R., Su, S., and Doherty, W. (1990). Divorce, remarriage, and substance abuse: A longitudinal study. *Journal of Marriage and the Family*, 52 (February), 157–169.

Pruett, M. K., Arthur, L., & Ebling, R. (2007). The hand that rocks the cradle: Maternal gatekeeping after divorce. *Pace University Law Review*, 27(4), 709–739.

Pruett, M.K., Cowan, C.P., Cowan, P.A., Diamond J.S. (2014), Supporting Father Involvement in the Context of Separation and Divorce, In K. Kuehnle, & L. Drozd (Eds.), *Parenting Plan Evaluations: Applied Research for the Family Court*. Oxford University Press, 123 – 154.

Pruett, M. K., McIntosh, J. E., & Kelly, J. B. (2014). Parental separation and overnight care of young children, part i: Consensus through theoretical and empirical integration. *Family Court Review*, 52, 240–255.

Roseby, V., & Johnston, J. R. (1998). Children of Armageddon: Common developmental threats in high-conflict divorcing families. *Child Adolesc Psychiatr Clin N Am*, 7, 295–309.

Sandler, I., Miles, J., Cookston, J., & Braver, S. (2008). Effects of father and mother parenting on children's mental health in high- and low-conflict divorces. *Family Court Review*, 46, 282–296.

Sandler, I. N., Wheeler, L. A., & Braver, S. L. (2013). Relations of parenting quality, interparental conflict, and overnights with mental health problems of children in divorcing families with high legal conflict. *Journal of Family Psychology*, 27(6), 915–924.

Thompson, P. (1998). Adolescents from families of divorce: Vulnerability to physiological and psychological disturbances. *J Psychosoc Nurs Ment Health Serv*, 36(3), 34–39.

Wallerstein J. S., & Blakeslee S. (1989). *Second Chances: Men, Women and Children a Decade after Divorce*. Ticknor & Fields.

Wolchik, S. A., Sandler, I. N., Millsap, R. E., Plummer, B. A., Greener, S. M., Anderson, E. R., Dawson-McClure, S. R., Hipke, K., & Haine, R. A. (2002). Six-year followup of preventive interventions for children of divorce: A randomized controlled trial. *Journal of the American Medical Association*, 288.

World Family Map: *Mapping Family Change and Child Well-Being Outcomes* (2014), International Report from Child Trends, www.worldfamilymap.org/2014.

Glossary of Legal Terms

Note: The following definitions are intended to be helpful, BUT they are not intended to constitute legal advice or address every possible meaning of the term(s) contained in this glossary.

50/50 Custody (or Equal Custody)
This is not a technical term. The term "custody" is no longer used in many areas, but parents may refer to a "50/50" or "equal custody" arrangement related to decision-making and physical custody. Most people stating "50/50" mean equal time (182.5 days per year). Professionals (for example, attorneys, custody evaluators, mediators, and judges) generally refer to this arrangement as "parental responsibility" or "decision making" and "visitation" or "shared physical custody."

Abuse
See domestic violence.

Action
A proceeding in a court of law. Can also be called **case, suit,** or **lawsuit**.

Advocate
Someone who helps and supports another person. An advocate will "take sides" and promote his or her client's views or interests.

Affidavit
A written statement of fact signed and sworn to before a person having authority to administer an oath.

Agreement
A complete understanding between both parties. You can agree

on one issue or many. If you reach an agreement with the other side on all issues, you can ask the judge for a hearing to make your agreement an Order.

Alienation (or Parental Alienation)
Any situation where one parent deliberately damages, and in some cases destroys, the previously healthy loving relationship between the child and the child's other parent, usually during divorce or a custody dispute.

Alimony
The money allowance one spouse must pay another by order of court during or after a divorce action.

Allegations
The assertions, declarations, or statements made in a pleading stating what the party expects to prove.

Alternative Dispute Resolution (ADR)
ADR is the common name for the different ways of settling a disagreement outside the courtroom. ADR includes mediation, arbitration, early neutral evaluations, parenting coordination, and settlement conference.

Annulment
The voiding of an act, such as a marriage.

Appeal
The process by which a case is brought from one court to a higher court for the case to be reviewed.

Arbitration
A neutral third party called an arbitrator hears arguments, reviews evidence and make a decision. This is different from mediation where the parties, not the mediator, make the decisions.

Attorney

A person with special education and training in the field of law who is licensed to practice law in the region where they practice. An attorney is the only person who is allowed to give you legal advice.

Best Interest of the Child

In deciding custody or parenting time and parenting responsibilities, the court must consider only those facts that directly affect the well-being of the child.

Central Governmental Depository

The office of the clerk of court that is responsible for collecting and disbursing court-ordered alimony and child support payments. The depository keeps payment records and files judgments if support is not paid.

Child support

The financial obligation that both parents have to their child(ren). Each region has a formula or means to determine how much money is paid from one parent to the other for the benefit of their dependent or minor child(ren).

Clerk of the Court

An officer of a court whose principal duty is to maintain court records.

Collaborative Law

An alternative way to settle disputes in which both parties hire specially trained attorneys who work to help them respectfully resolve their conflicts outside of court. The participants agree to work together to seek a solution that works for both parties. If the dispute can't be resolved through the collaborative process, or if one of the parties threatens to go to court, then the collaborative law process ends and neither lawyer can continue to work on the case.

Confidential
Information that shall not be disclosed except under named conditions.

Contempt
Disregarding or disobeying a court order. It is a very serious thing to be held in contempt of court.

Custody
The rights and responsibilities between parents for their child(ren). The custody and visitation or parenting plan must describe the legal custody and physical custody that is in the child(ren)'s best interests. Also see Parental Responsibility, Parenting Time, and Time-Sharing.

Custody Evaluator
A court appointed expert who is educated, experienced and trained in child development and the effects of divorce or separation on children. The custody evaluator (or investigator) assesses a family and recommends to the judge a parenting plan that is in the best interests of the children.

Custody and Visitation (or Parenting Plan)
The plan describing how the parents will be involved in their child(ren)'s life, recognizing that children of different ages have different needs and that the plan will also change if one or both of the parents move. A parenting plan usually describes the child(ren)'s schedule and describes which parent will make decisions about various things in the child(ren)'s life.

Delinquent
Late.

Dependent Child(ren)

Children who depend on their parent(s) for support either because they are under the age of 18, they have a mental or physical disability that prevents them from supporting themselves, or they are in high school while between the ages of 18 and 19.

Deposition

Testimony taken under oath outside the courtroom concerning the facts and circumstances surrounding an incident, recorded by a court reporter. The deposition may be introduced as evidence in court.

Discovery

A pre-trial procedure that allows each party to get written or oral information from the other party.

Dissolution of Marriage

Divorce; a court action to end a marriage.

Divorce

The ending of a marriage by a court order. Also see Dissolution of Marriage.

Docket

The order in which the court will hear cases. The list often is posted outside the courtroom with cases listed by the petitioner's name in civil court and the defendant's name in criminal court.

Domestic Violence or Abuse (See Intimate Partner Violence also)

Violence or abuse is a pattern of behavior used to establish power and control over another person through fear and intimidation, often including the threat or actual use of violence. Abuse of family members can take many forms, including emotional abuse, economic abuse, sexual abuse, using children, threats, intimidation, isolation, and a variety of other behaviors used to maintain fear, intimidation and power. In most areas, you can get a Domestic Violence Protective Order (or No Contact Order) if you have a "household" relationship with the other party and he/she committed a crime of domestic violence against you, such as assault, burglary, criminal trespass, criminal mischief, terroristic threatening, violating a domestic violence order, or harassment.

Early Neutral Evaluation
Early neutral evaluation provides parties in a dispute with an early and frank evaluation of the merits of their case by an objective, neutral evaluator. The evaluator is not a decision-maker.

Evidence
Information provided to the court by the parties during the course of a case to assist in the decision making process. This can include testimony, documents and other materials.

Ex Parte
Communication with the judge by only one party. If you have something you wish to tell the judge, you should ask for a hearing or file information in the clerk of court's office, with certification that a copy was sent to the other party.

Family/Household Member
Spouses, former spouses, persons related by blood or marriage, persons who are presently residing together as if a family or who have resided together in the past as if a family, and persons who are parents of a child in common regardless of whether they have been married. With the exception of persons who

have a child in common, the family or household members must be currently residing or have in the past resided together in the same single dwelling unit. (See also Domestic Violence or Abuse)

Filing
Delivering a petition, response, motion, or other pleading in a court case to the clerk of court's office.

Final Judgment
A written document signed by a judge that contains the judge's decision in your case.

Financial Affidavit
A sworn statement that contains information regarding your income, expenses, assets, and liabilities.

Finding
The court's decision.

Guardian ad Litem (GAL)
An attorney or special advocate appointed by the court to investigate your child's situation, and file a report with the court about what is in the best interest of your child(ren). Guards do not "work for" either party. The guard may interview the parties, visit their homes, visit the child(ren)'s school(s) and speak with teachers, or use other resources to make their recommendation.

Hearing
A legal proceeding before a judge or designated officer on a motion. The judge may hear evidence and make a decision about an issue in your case.

In Camera
Literally means "in chambers." A hearing or discussion with the judge in the privacy of his or her office.

Injunction
Writ or order by a court prohibiting a specific action from being carried out by a person. A preliminary injunction is granted until a full hearing can be held to determine if it should be made permanent.

Intimate Partner Violence (IPV)
Intimate partner violence (IPV) is defined as threatened, attempted, or completed physical or sexual violence or emotional abuse by a current or former intimate partner. IPV can be committed by a spouse, an ex-spouse, a current or former boyfriend or girlfriend, or a dating partner. **(See also Domestic Violence or Abuse.)**

Joint Custody
See shared physical custody and 50/50 Custody.

Joint Legal Custody
Both parents have the responsibility for making the major life decisions affecting the child's welfare, such as where the child(ren) go(es) to the doctor or goes to school. The alternative to shared legal custody is sole legal custody. There is also physical custody. (See parenting plans and 50/50 custody for more information.)

Judge
An elected or government appointed official who is responsible for deciding matters on which you and the other parties in your case are unable to agree. A judge is a neutral person who is responsible for ensuring that your case is resolved in a manner which is fair, equitable, and legal.

Judicial Assistant (JA)
The judge's personal staff assistant.

Judgment
A final determination by a court of the rights and claims of the parties in an action.

Jurisdiction
Courts within a particular geographic area.

Legal Custody
The right and obligation to make major life decisions such as where the child goes to school or which doctors he or she sees. There are two types of legal custody: joint legal custody and sole legal custody.

Mediator
A person who is trained and certified to assist parties in reaching an agreement before going to court. Mediators do not take either party's side and are not allowed to give legal advice.

Mediation-Arbitration (Med-Arb)
Mediation-Arbitration is a combination of mediation and arbitration. Parties work to come up with their own agreements, but give a neutral third party the authority to make a decision if mediation is not successful. In some areas, a Med-Arb model of Parenting Coordination is used instead of the Integrated Model of Parenting Coordination. See Parenting Coordination, Integrated Model.

Modification/Modify
To change an existing court order because of a change in circumstances.

Motion
An oral or written request for an action made by a party before, during, or after a trial, upon which a court issues a ruling or order.

No Contact Order

A court order directing a party not to speak to, call, send mail to, visit, or go near his or her spouse, ex-spouse, child(ren), or other family member. Also see Protective Order.

Notice

A written order to appear in court at a certain time and place.

Oath

A solemn affirmation to tell the truth.

Order

A command or direction given by a judge. An order can be in writing or spoken. Violating a court order is very serious and can result in being held in contempt or sanctioned in other ways.

Parenting Coordination, Integrated Model

The *Integrated Model of Parenting Coordination* is a hybrid psychological-legal model that incorporates knowledge and skills from the legal, mental health, and mediation professions. It is an alternative dispute resolution (ADR) process for parents (separated, divorced or never married) who are unable to resolve parenting disputes with a goal of helping parents resolve their conflicts without harm to their child(ren).

Parenting Plan (Custody and Visitation Plan)

A document that describes how parents will be involved with and make decisions regarding their minor child(ren). The plan contains a time-sharing schedule for the parents and child(ren). The issues concerning the minor child(ren) may include, but are not limited to, the child(ren)'s education, health care, and physical, social, and emotional well-being. In creating the plan, all circumstances between the parties, including the parties' historic relationship, domestic violence, and other factors are taken into consideration. The parenting plan is developed and agreed to by the parents and approved by a court or, if the parents cannot agree, set by the court.

Party
A person involved in a court case, either as a petitioner or respondent.

Paternity Testing
A medical test to determine who is the father of a child.

Petitioner
A person who starts a case by submitting a petition or written request to the court for legal action. In family cases, the terms petitioner and respondent are used.

Physical Custody
The right of a parent to have the child(ren) live in their home. There are generally two types of physical custody arrangements: primary physical custody and shared physical custody.

Pleading
Formal written allegations by the parties in a lawsuit of their respective claims and defenses; pleadings are filed with the court.

Primary Physical Custody (or Primary Residence)
The home in which the child(ren) spends most of his/her time. This is a technical term that should be applied only after the parents have decided on what the best overall schedule, or parenting plan, is for their child(ren).

Pro Se Litigant
A person who appears in court without the assistance of a lawyer.

Privileged Communication
Statements and conversations made under circumstances of

assured confidentiality that must not be disclosed except under certain conditions.

Pro Bono
Literally "for the good"; when an attorney represents the party for free.

Protective Order
A court order which is meant to protect a person from another person. Also see No Contact Order.

Reasonable Visitation
This is not a technical term, but often refers to a specific schedule for contact between a parent and child(ren) that is designed to encourage a close and continuing relationship with due regard for education commitments of child(ren), any health or social factors of the child(ren), business and personal commitments of both parents, and home arrangements of both parents. See Shared (or Joint) Physical Custody and Shared (or Joint) Parental Responsibility.

Record
A copy of the pleadings, exhibits, orders, or decrees filed in a case in the trial court and a transcript of the testimony taken in the case.

Respondent
The person who responds to the petitioner. If you did not file the petition to start a court case, and you are named in the case, you are the respondent. In family matters, the terms petitioner and respondent are used.

Rotating Custody
This is not a technical term, but is often used to refer to a parental time-sharing plan in which the child(ren) live with each

parent approximately one-half of the time. This term generally refers to physical custody of child(ren) after divorce, which is alternated between the mother and father at specific periods of time, as determined by the court. See also Joint Legal Custody, Shared Parental Responsibility, Shared Physical Custody, 50/50 Custody, and Parenting Plans for more information.

Service
The delivery or communication of a legal document in a suit to the opposite party.

Settlement
The termination of a civil case before trial by the agreement between the parties.

Settlement Conference (in some areas called a Case Management or Status Conference)
A settlement conference is a meeting with a judge before trial to explore ways to settle your issues. The meeting includes both parties and your lawyers (if you have them). The judge's role is to try to help you reach an agreement, but is not a decision-maker.

Shared Parental Responsibility
A court-ordered relationship in which both parents retain full parental rights and responsibilities with respect to their child and in which both parents confer with each other so that major decisions affecting the welfare of the child will be determined jointly. Also see Joint Legal Custody.

Shared Physical Custody
The technical term for when the child(ren) live(s) with each parent. The amount of time a child may live with each parent may vary widely depending on the best interest of the child(ren) and the laws in a particular area. See parenting plans and 50/50 custody for more information.

Sole Legal Custody (or Sole Parental Responsibility)

One parent is give the legal authority to make the major life decisions affecting the child's welfare, such as where the child(ren) goes to the doctor or goes to school. If the parents do not agree on a decision about the child(ren), the parent with sole legal custody has the right to make the final decision. The alternative to sole legal custody is joint legal custody.

Statutes (Laws)

Laws made by the legislature, as opposed to case law or unwritten common laws.

Subpoena

A written order issued by the court requiring an individual to come and talk under oath in court. Subpoenas can also require a person to bring to court specific documents or other items.

Supervised Visitation

A parenting arrangement under which visitation between a parent and his or her child(ren) is supervised by either a friend, family member, or a supervised visitation center.

Temporary Order (or Interim Order)

A temporary order is any order made in a case for the final order is made. These are generally short-term decisions by the judge about child support, child custody, visitation, possession of the family home, attorney fees, spousal support or the payment of debts until a final court order can be issued.

Testimony

Any statement made by a witness under oath in a legal proceeding.

Time-Sharing Schedule

A timetable included in the parenting plan that specifies the time, including overnights and holidays that a minor child will spend with each parent. If developed and agreed to by the parents of a minor child, the court must approve it. If the parents cannot agree, the court will establish the schedule. See Visitation also.

Trial

Formal court proceeding at which evidence is heard and the case is decided.

Visitation (Time-Sharing Schedule)

The right of a parent and child to contact and visit one another when the child is residing or visiting with the other parent. The law presumes that it is in the best interests of the child(ren) to have frequent and continuing contact with both parents so that both parents can maintain a good relationship with the child(ren). The schedule for visitation will be set out in the parenting or custody and visitation plan. See parenting plans for more information.

Waiver

The voluntary giving up of a privilege or right.

Witness

Any person called to testify under oath in a criminal or civil proceeding regarding what that person has seen, heard, or otherwise observed.

About the Author

Debra K. Carter, PhD is a clinical and forensic psychologist, and the co-founder and clinical director of the National Cooperative Parenting Center. She is author of the professional text, *Parenting Coordination*, along with numerous academic and professional articles. She is a Qualified Parenting  Coordinator and internationally recognized expert in Parenting Coordination and alternative dispute resolution. Dr. Carter has presented as an invited speaker at numerous national and international family law conferences. She has trained professionals and worked with families during and after divorce across the United States and in Europe. Dr. Carter has received numerous awards and honors for her clinical work and contributions to the family law system, including "Psychologist of the Year" and recognition as a "Distinguished Psychologist." She is also the mother of three children.

More Great Books from
Unhooked Books

The Complicated Relationships Publisher

Available in paperback and in ebook (digital)
format from booksellers
everywhere

Visit our online bookstore at
www.unhookedbooks.com
Or call 1-888-986-4665

CPSIA information can be obtained at www.ICGtesting.com
Printed in the USA
LVOW04s1011080415

433751LV00003B/3/P

9 781936 268887